The Princeton Review

Math Workout for the SAT

By Cornelia Cocke

First Edition
Random House, Inc.
New York

www.PrincetonReview.com

The Independent Education Consultants Association recognizes The Princeton Review as a valuable resource for high school and college students applying to college and graduate school.

The Princeton Review, Inc.
2315 Broadway
New York, NY 10024
E-mail: booksupport@review.com

ISBN: 0-375-76433-X
ISSN: 1551-6431

SAT and Scholastic Assessment Test are registered trademarks of the College Entrance Examination Board.

Editor: Allegra Viner
Updated by: Doug Pierce
Production Editor: Patricia Dublin
Production Coordinator: Stephanie J. Martin

Manufactured in the United States of America on partially recycled paper.

9 8 7 6 5 4

First Edition

ACKNOWLEDGMENTS

I would like to thank Chris Kensler, Kristin Fayne-Mulroy, Laurice Pearson, Jane Lacher, Jeannie Yoon, Meher Khambata, and Andrea Gordon for their invaluable help, editing skills, and overall perspicacity. Special thanks to Doug Pierce, Allegra Viner, Patricia Dublin, Stephanie Martin, and Ellen Mendlow. For additional production and editing help, thanks to Andrea Paykin, Andy Lutz, Lee Elliott, Cynthia Brantley, Julian Ham, Peter Jung, Andrew Dunn, Clayton Harding, Kathleen Standard, Jefferson Nichols, Sara Kane, Ramsey Silberberg, Matthew Clark, Dinica Quesada, Carol Slominski, Christopher D. Scott, and Maria Dente. Special thanks also to Christine Parker and the Diagpalooza team.

Special thanks to Adam Robinson, who conceived of and perfected the Joe Bloggs approach to standardized tests and many of the other successful techniques used by The Princeton Review.

CONTENTS

Introduction

IN THE BEGINNING . . .

Even though the SAT is designed for juniors and seniors, most of the math on the test bears little resemblance to the type of math found in the high school classroom. Many students find it hard to believe—not to mention a little humiliating—that a test that seems so difficult actually tests little more than basic algebra, arithmetic, and geometry. Even students who are very good at math in school often have trouble on the SAT. Why?

The fact is that while the SAT uses basic mathematical concepts, it's unlike any math test you will ever see in school. The SAT uses basic math problems in very particular ways. This is why preparing for the SAT requires a new set of skills. The SAT does not test how smart you are, how well you will do in school, or what kind of person you are. It only tests *how well you do on the SAT*. And doing well on the SAT is a skill that can be learned.

How can you improve your score on the SAT? First, you need to learn the structure of the test. This will help you develop an overall test-taking strategy. Then you need to learn some powerful test-taking skills, which will help you think your way through SAT-type problems.

Some of our advice may sound a little strange. In fact, if you try some of our techniques in math class, your teacher will probably be unhappy. But remember: This isn't math class. This is the SAT, and it's your job to get as good at SAT math as you can.

STRUCTURE OF THE MATH SECTIONS

Of the nine multiple-choice sections on the SAT, three of them will be math. The questions will be presented in two different formats: regular multiple choice and grid-ins. We will discuss how to deal with each of these question formats.

HOW TO USE THIS BOOK

This book is designed for students who want concentrated math preparation. It can be used alone or as a supplement to our *Cracking the New SAT*. While we will briefly review the essential Princeton Review test-taking strategies and problem-solving skills. If you want an in-depth guide to these techniques, you'll want to also read *Cracking the New SAT*.

WHERE DOES THE SAT COME FROM?

The SAT is published by the Educational Testing Service (ETS) under the sponsorship of the College Entrance Examination Board (the College Board). ETS and the College Board are both private companies. We'll tell you more about them in Chapter 1.

WHAT IS THE PRINCETON REVIEW?

The Princeton Review is one of the nation's fastest-growing test-preparation companies. We have conducted courses in hundreds of locations around the country, and we prepare more students for the SAT than anyone else. We also prepare students for the PSAT/NMSQT, ACT, GRE, GMAT, LSAT, MCAT, and other standardized tests.

The Princeton Review's techniques are unique and powerful. We developed them after spending countless hours scrutinizing real SATs, analyzing them with computers, and proving our theories with real students. Our methods have been widely imitated, but no one else achieves our score improvements.

This book is based on our extensive experience in the classroom. Our techniques for cracking the SAT will help you improve your SAT scores by teaching you to:

1. think like the test writers at ETS

2. take full advantage of the limited time allowed

3. find the answers to questions you don't understand by guessing intelligently

4. avoid the traps that ETS has laid for you (and use those traps to your advantage)

1 Strategies

We'll say it again: This isn't the kind of test you get in math class. You need some special techniques for handling SAT problems—techniques that will help you go faster and that take advantage of the format of the questions. Some of the things we suggest may seem awkward at first, so practice them. If you do the math questions on the SAT the way your math teacher taught you, you waste time and throw away points.

ORDER OF DIFFICULTY

To formulate an overall test-taking strategy, the most important thing to learn is the order of difficulty of the math sections. The questions on your SAT are selected with extreme care, in the same way, every time. Knowing how the test is put together is crucial for scoring well. The chart on the next page shows you how the questions are organized on each of the math sections.

As you can see, sections are arranged in order of difficulty, with the easy questions at the beginning, medium questions in the middle, and the hard questions at the end of each section. It is crucial to know the difficulty of a question in order to know the best way to solve it. This is so important that the exercises in this book provide an easy, a medium, and a hard question for each major question type. We've kept the question numbers consistent to help you learn which questions are easy, medium, and hard.

JOE BLOGGS

Joe Bloggs is our name for the average SAT tester. Joe isn't stupid—he's just average. He takes this test as he would take a math test in school, and he gets an average score. If you learn how Joe takes this test, you can learn how to take it better.

When Joe takes the SAT, he makes two important mistakes. First, he tries to finish the test. This encourages him to rush through the easy problems, which he should get right, but he makes silly mistakes because he's rushing. He rushes all the way into the hard problems, getting almost no questions right. Why? Because of Joe's second mistake: He thinks that he can solve every problem in a straightforward way. While this works on the easy problems, the hard problems are full of trap answers, which cause Joe to spend too much time on each question or pick the wrong choice.

How can you avoid being like Joe? First, learn to do the right number of problems. Second, learn some test-taking techniques that will make harder problems much easier and help you avoid the traps that the test writers have laid for you.

PACING

Almost everybody works too fast on the SAT, losing a lot of points due to careless errors. The SAT isn't your usual math situation—you don't get *partial credit* for "having the right idea." The only thing that matters is what you bubble in on your answer sheet. Slow down! If you find yourself making careless mistakes, you are throwing points out the window.

Unless you're shooting for a score of 700 or above, do not finish the math sections. Again, this isn't like math class. The test isn't designed for you to finish, and you'll hurt your score by trying to do so. If you miss a total of around five or six questions for all three sections, you're probably hitting the right pace. More mistakes than that, and you're going too quickly. If you aren't missing any questions but aren't finishing, you should guess more aggressively and try to work a bit faster.

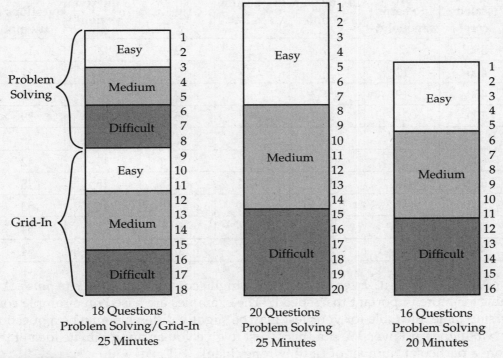

18 Questions	20 Questions	16 Questions
Problem Solving/Grid-In	Problem Solving	Problem Solving
25 Minutes	25 Minutes	20 Minutes

SCORING

If you were betting your hard-earned cash, wouldn't you want to know the odds? On the SAT, you're betting for more points, and it's important to understand how the scoring works so you'll play smart.

For each right answer, you earn one raw point. For each wrong answer, you lose one-quarter of a raw point. That's it. If you leave a question blank, nothing happens either way, except that the total number of points you can earn is reduced.

Every right answer earns you one point, whether it's easy or hard.

That's important to understand, because most people spend too much time on hard questions. They aren't going to do anything more for you than easy questions—and you'll hurt your score if you miss easy or medium questions because you're rushing to finish.

Based on a sample conversion table, here are some examples of what you have to do to get a particular score—there are a total of 54 math questions.

To get (scaled score)	You need to earn: (raw points)	Attempt this many questions				
		20-question section	10-question section	Grid-Ins	15-question section	Total # of questions to attempt
350	7	6	2	2	2	12
400	12	7	3	3	4	17
450	19	9	4	4	6	23
500	25	11	5	5	8	29
550	32	14	6	6	10	36
600	38	16	6	7	13	42
650	44	18	7	8	15	48
700	47	all	all	9	all	53
750	52	all	all	all	all	54
800	54	all	all	all	all	54

Amazing, isn't it? Even to get a very high score, *you don't have to finish.* Accuracy is more important than speed! (The examples are based on a sample conversion table; the table for your test may be slightly different—maybe a question or two higher or lower. We put this in just to give you an approximate idea of the score a particular number of right/wrong/blank will give you.)

GUESSING

Say you start to work on a problem and get stuck. Should you just move on? Not if you can cross out any of the wrong answer choices. Are you working on a hard problem? Then cross out any obvious answers and guess from what's left. Are you working on an easy question? Go with your instincts.

If you can eliminate even one answer choice, guess.

Why? Because if you guessed randomly on five questions, without eliminating anything (let your pet monkey pick the answer), you'd have a one out of five chance of picking a right answer. That one right answer earns you (or your pet monkey) one raw point, and the four wrong answers cost you $4 \times \frac{1}{4}$ of a point subtracted. You break even. Eliminating one or more answer choices improves your odds considerably—so take advantage of it!

WHEN TO GUESS

All of that said, we don't mean to suggest that you skip merrily through the sections guessing with abandon. There are smart places to guess and not-so-smart places to guess.

Always be aware of where you are in the section. Use the order-of-difficulty information to guide your guessing: easy questions = easy answers; hard questions = hard answers.

GOOD GUESS

- Geometry, drawn to scale. If you can approximate the length or area or angle measurement, go for it. Applies to easy, medium, and hard questions.

- Any grid-in you've got an answer for. No penalty for wrong answers.

BAD GUESS

- Obvious answers on hard questions

- Long, complicated word problems at the end of the section. (Spend your time on something shorter and more manageable.)

- Questions you don't have time to read.

CALCULATORS

Seems like a good deal, doesn't it? Well, maybe. It depends on the problem. Don't grab your calculator too quickly—you have to know how solve the problem first.

Calculators can only calculate; they can't think. You need to figure out how to solve the problem before you can begin calculating.

Calculators are great for helping you avoid silly mistakes in your arithmetic, and you should use them when you can. They can help ensure that you make correct calculations, but they can't tell you which calculations are the right ones to make. So be sure you figure out how to solve the problem before you start punching numbers into your calculator.

Think before you punch.

TIPS TO CALCULATOR HAPPINESS

- Get a calculator that follows the order of operations and has keys for x^2, y^x, and $\sqrt{}$.

- Use the same calculator every time you practice SAT problems.

- Estimate your answer first.

- Check each number after you punch it in.

CARELESS MISTAKES

If you are prone to careless mistakes—and most of us are—you probably make the same kinds of careless mistakes over and over. If you take the time to analyze the questions you get wrong, you will discover which kinds are your personal favorites. Then you can compensate for them when you take the SAT.

In the world, and in math class, it's most important for you to understand concepts and ways to solve problems. On the SAT, it's most important that you bubble in the correct answer. Students typically lose anywhere from 30 to 100 points simply by making careless, preventable mistakes.

Some common mistakes to watch for:

- misreading the question

- computation error

- punching in the wrong thing on the calculator

- on a medium or hard question, stopping after one or two steps, when the question requires three or four steps

- failing to estimate first

- answering a different question from the one asked

If, for example, you find you keep missing questions because you multiply wrong, then do every multiplication twice. Do every step on paper, not in your head. If you make a lot of mistakes on positive/negative, write out each step, and be extra careful on those questions. Correcting careless mistakes is an easy way to pick up more points, so make sure you analyze your mistakes so you know what to look out for.

PLUGGING IN

One of the most powerful math techniques on the SAT is called Plugging In. The idea of Plugging In is to take all of the variables—things like x, y, z—in a problem and replace them with actual numbers. This turns your algebra problems into simple arithmetic and can make even the hardest problem into an easy one.

HOW TO RECOGNIZE A PLUGGING-IN QUESTION

- There are variables in the answer choices.

- The question says something like *in terms of x . . . .*

- Your first thought is to write an equation.

- The question asks for a percentage or fractional part of something, but doesn't give you any actual amounts.

HOW TO SOLVE A PLUGGING-IN QUESTION

- Don't write an equation.

- Pick an easy number and substitute it for the variable.

- Work the problem through and get an answer. Circle it so you don't lose track of it.

- Plug in your number—the one you chose in the beginning—to the answer choices and see which choice produces your circled answer.

Here's an example:

Jill spent x dollars on pet toys and 12 dollars on socks. If the amount Jill spent was twice the amount she earns each week, how much does Jill earn each week in terms of x?

(A) $2(x + 12)$

(B) $2x + 24$

(C) $\dfrac{x}{2} + 12$

(D) $\dfrac{x + 12}{2}$

(E) $\dfrac{x - 12}{2}$

Solution: Let's plug in 100 for x. That means Jill spent a total of 112 dollars. If that was twice her weekly salary, then she makes half of 112, or 56 dollars a week. Circle 56. Now we plug our number, 100, into the answers to see which one gives us 56. (A) 2(100 + 12) = 224. No good. (B) is 224, which is also too big.

(C) 50 + 12 = 62 (D) $\frac{112}{2}$ = 56! Yes! (E) is $\frac{88}{2}$ = 44. Nope. The answer is D.

Here's a harder example:

> Karl bought x bags of red marbles for y dollars per bag, and z bags of blue marbles for $3y$ dollars per bag. If he bought twice as many bags of blue marbles as red marbles, then in terms of y, what was the average cost, in dollars, per bag of marbles?

(A) $\frac{3y}{2}$

(B) $\frac{7y}{3}$

(C) $3y - y$

(D) $2y$

(E) $6y$

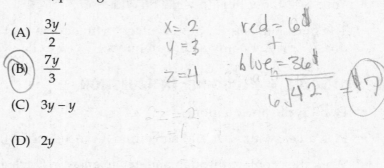

Solution: You don't really want to do the algebra, do you? Let's use simple, low numbers and plug in. How about $x = 2$ and $y = 3$? That's 2 bags of red marbles at $3 each. So he spent $6 on red marbles. (In word problems, it helps to keep track of what the numbers represent.) If he bought twice as many bags of blue marbles, then $z = 4$. So he bought 4 bags of blue marbles at $3y$ or $9 a can and spent a total of $36. Now we figure the average price by adding up the dollars spent and dividing that by the total number of bags. He spent $6 + $36 = $42 on 2 + 4 = 6 bags of marbles. So the average price per bag is $\frac{42}{6}$ = $7. Circle $7.

Now, since we said $y = 3$, plug 3 in for y in the answer choices and see which one gives you 7. (A) gives us $\frac{9}{2}$, so we can eliminate it. (B) is 7, so that's the answer.

Here's a different kind of example:

At his bake sale, Mr. Heftwhistle sold 30% of his pies to one friend. Mr. Heftwhistle then sold 60% of the remaining pies to another friend. What percent of his original number of pies did Mr. Heftwhistle have left?

(A) 10%
(B) 18%
(C) 28%
(D) 36%
(E) 40%

Solution: If you don't plug in, you may make the sad mistake of picking (A) or of working with ugly fractions. Plugging in a number is much easier. Let's say Mr. Heftwhistle had 100 pies. 30% of 100 equals 30, so he's left with 70. 60% of 70 equals 42, so he's left with 28. Here's the great thing about plugging in 100 on percentage problems—28 (left) out of 100 (original number) is simply 28%. That's it. (C) is the answer.

TIPS FOR PLUGGING IN HAPPINESS

- Pick easy numbers like 2, 4, 10, 100. The best number to choose depends on the question: Use 100 for percents.

- Avoid picking 0, 1, or any number that shows up in the answer choices.

- If the number you picked leads to ugly computations—fractions, negatives, or anything you need a calculator for—bail out and pick an easier number.

- Practice!

On the next page is a Quick Quiz, so you can practice Plugging In before you continue. The question number corresponds to the difficulty level in the 25-question multiple-choice section. Answers and explanations immediately follow every Quick Quiz.

QUICK QUIZ #1

EASY

6. If p is an odd integer, which of the following must also be an odd integer?

    (A) $p + 1$ = 4 $p = 3$

    (B) $\dfrac{p}{2}$ $\dfrac{3}{2}$

    (C) $p + 2$ 5

    (D) $2p$ 6

    (E) $p - 1$ 2

MEDIUM

13. If $\dfrac{y}{3} = 6x$, then in terms of y, $x =$

    $y = 36$

    (A) $3y$

    $\dfrac{36}{3} = 6x$

    (B) $2y$

    $12 = 6x$

    (C) y

    $2 = x$

    (D) $\dfrac{y}{2}$

    (E) $\dfrac{y}{18}$

HARD

24. Mary spilled $\dfrac{2}{5}$ of her peanuts, and Jessica ate $\dfrac{1}{3}$ of what was left. Jessica then gave the peanuts to Max and Sam, who each ate half of what remained. What fractional part of Mary's peanuts did Sam eat?

    (A) $\dfrac{1}{15}$ 100

    (B) $\dfrac{1}{10}$ 60

    -20

    (C) $\dfrac{1}{5}$ 40

    (D) $\dfrac{1}{3}$ M 20 S 20 $\dfrac{20}{100} = \dfrac{1}{5}$

    (E) $\dfrac{4}{5}$

ANSWERS AND EXPLANATIONS: QUICK QUIZ #1

6. **C** p has to be odd. Let's make $p = 3$. Try that in the answer choices, and cross out anything that isn't odd. (A): $3 + 1 = 4$. Cross out (A). (B): $\frac{3}{2}$. Cross out (B). (Fractions can't be odd or even.) (C): $3 + 2 = 5$, leave (C) in. (D): $2(3) = 6$. Cross out (D). (E): $3 - 1 = 2$. Cross out (E). Only (C) works.

13. **E** Plug in $y = 36$, which makes $x = 2$. Now we plug in 36 for y in the answer choices and look for x, which is 2. (A): something huge. (B): still something huge. (C): 36. (D): $\frac{36}{2} = 18$, still too big. (E): $\frac{36}{18} = 2$, so (E) is correct.

24. **C** On this kind of question, there aren't variables in the answer choices, but there's an *implied* variable in the question because we don't know how many peanuts Mary started with. Let's say she had 10 ounces of peanuts. (The "ounces" doesn't really matter—it's the number that's important.) If she spilled $\frac{2}{5}$ of 10, she spilled 4, leaving her with 6. If Jessica ate $\frac{1}{3}$ of 6, she ate 2, leaving Mary with 4. If Max and Sam split 4, they each ate 2. The fractional part is $\frac{\text{part}}{\text{whole}}$, so Sam's fractional part is $\frac{2}{10}$ or $\frac{1}{5}$. (Whew.)

A tree diagram makes this easier to deal with:

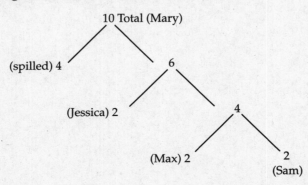

In question 12, you may have had a hard time coming up with numbers that worked evenly. That's OK—it takes practice. You can plug in any numbers you want, as long as they satisfy the conditions of the problem, so you might as well plug in numbers that are easy to work with.

In question 19, you could solve this without plugging in, but then you're dealing with fractional parts of a whole, the whole being Mary's peanuts. It's very easy to get confused doing it that way, because the numbers aren't concrete and they quickly become meaningless. The advantage of Plugging In is that you're working with actual amounts, just like real life. One more thing: We picked 10 because the first thing we had to do was take $\frac{2}{5}$ of it. If we'd picked a number we couldn't take $\frac{2}{5}$ of easily, we would have tried another number.

PLUGGING IN THE ANSWER CHOICES

Good news. Unlike the math tests you usually have in school, the SAT is primarily multiple choice. That means that on many problems, you don't have to generate your own answer to a problem. Instead, the answer will be one of the five answers sitting on the page right in front of you. All you have to figure out is *which* one of the five is the answer.

HOW TO RECOGNIZE QUESTIONS FOR PLUGGING IN THE ANSWER CHOICES

- The question will be straightforward—something like "How old is Bob?" or "How many potatoes are in the bag?" or "What was the original cost of the stereo?"

- The answer choices will be actual values.

How to Plug In the Answer Choices

Don't write an equation. Instead, pick an answer and work it through the steps of the problem, one at a time, and see if it works. In essence, you're asking *what if C is the answer? Does that solve the problem?*

Here's an example:

If $\left[\dfrac{3(x-1)}{2} = \dfrac{9}{x-2} \right]$, what is the value of x?

$$\frac{3(0)}{2} = \frac{9}{-1}$$

(A) −4
(B) −2
(C) 1
(D) 4
(E) 9

$$\frac{3(3)}{2} = \frac{9}{2}$$

Solution: Let's try (C) first. We'll plug in 1 for x and see if the equation works:

$$\frac{3(1-1)}{2} = \frac{9}{1-2}$$

$$\frac{0}{2} = \frac{9}{-1}$$

Okay, so (C) isn't the answer. Cross it out. Let's try (D):

$$\frac{3(4-1)}{2} = \frac{9}{4-2}$$

$$\frac{9}{2} = \frac{9}{2}$$

The equation works, so (D) is the answer. Sure, we could have done the algebra, but wasn't plugging in easier? Once again, we've turned an algebra problem into an arithmetic problem, and all we have to do is manage simple operations like 4 − 1. You're much more likely to make mistakes dealing with x than with 4 − 1. Also, when you plug in, you're taking advantage of the fact that there are only five answer choices. One of them is correct. You might as well try them and find out which one it is—and you no longer have to face the horror of working out a problem algebraically and finding that your answer isn't one of the choices.

Here's a harder example:

> Paul had twice as many potatoes as Dan, who
> had the same number of potatoes as Zed. If
> Paul were to give five potatoes to Zed, then
> Dan would have three times as many potatoes
> as Paul. How many potatoes did Dan have?

(A) 10
(B) 6
(C) 3
(D) 2
(E) 1

[handwritten: P = 2D, D = Z, P−5 = 3P]

Solution: Let's try choice (C) first. If Dan started with 3, then Zed also started with 3. Since Paul had twice as many potatoes as Dan, then Paul started with 6. If he gives 5 to Zed, Paul now has 1 and Zed has 8. Dan still has 3 potatoes, which is three times as many as Paul. So (C) is the right answer. If (C) didn't work, we could keep trying until we found the answer that did.

To keep things organized, make a chart:

	D	Z	P
Originally:	3	3	6
After exchange:	3	8	1

[handwritten chart: D Z P / 3 3 6 / 3 8 1]

TIPS FOR HAPPINESS WHEN PLUGGING IN THE ANSWER CHOICES

- (C) is a good answer to try first, unless it's awkward to work with.

- The answers will be in numerical order, so you may be able to eliminate answers that are either too big or too small, based on the result you got with (C). If the answer to (C) was too small, you should try bigger answer choices. If the answer to (C) was too big, try smaller answer choices.

- Don't try to work out all the steps in advance—the nice thing about plugging in is that you do the steps one at a time.

- Plugging In questions may be long word problems or short arithmetic problems, and they can appear in the easy, medium, or difficult sections. The harder the question, the better off you'll be plugging in.

- Make a chart if you have a lot of stuff to keep track of.

QUICK QUIZ #2

EASY

6. If 4 less than the product of *b* and 6 is 44, what is the value of *b*?

    $(b \cdot 6) - 4 = 44$

    (A) 2
    (B) 4
    (C) 6
    (D) 8
    (E) 14

MEDIUM

13. A store reduces the price of a CD player by 20% and then reduces that price by 15%. If the final price of the CD player is $170, what was its original price?

    .20   .15

    (A) $140
    (B) $185
    (C) $200
    (D) $250
    (E) $275

HARD

20. Triangle *ABC* has sides measuring 2, 3, and *r*. Which of the following is a possible value for *r*?

    (A) 0.5
    (B) 1
    (C) 2
    (D) 5
    (E) 6

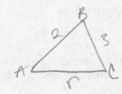

r=2

2 2 3

a+b>c

ANSWERS AND EXPLANATIONS: QUICK QUIZ #2

6. **D** Let's try (C) first, so $b = 6$. The product of 6 and 6 is 36, and 4 less than 36 is 32. 32 isn't 44—cross out (C). Let's try a higher number, (D). If $b = 8$, the product of 8 and 6 is 48, and 4 less than 48 is 44.

13. **D** Try (C) first. If the original price of the CD player was $200, then 20% of 200 is 40. That leaves us with a price of $160. Hey—the final price was $170, and we're already below that. We need a higher number. Try (D): If the original price was $250, take 20% of 250 = 50. Now the price is $200. Take another 15% ($30) off and we get 200 − 30 = 170.

20. **C** You need to know a rule here—the sum of any 2 sides of a triangle must equal more than the third side. Try (C) first. If $r = 2$, then the sides are 2, 2, 3. Add up any pair and you get a number that's higher than the remaining number. So it works. (Try some of the other answers, just for practice, and see how they *don't* work.)

Let's do a little analysis. See how the questions got harder as you went along? In the easy question, you had to read carefully, multiply, and subtract. In the medium question, you had to take percentages. In the hard question, you had to deal with geometry without a diagram and also know a particular rule. For all the questions, plugging in allowed you to avoid writing an equation. Less work is good.

ESTIMATING

A ROUGH ESTIMATE MAY BE ALL THAT'S NECESSARY

We like that. The less work the better. Maybe you'll only be able to eliminate a couple of answers. That's okay too.

For example:

> When .20202 is multiplied by 10^5 and then subtracted from 66,666, the result is
>
> (A) −46,464
> (B)   464.98
> (C)   4,646.4
> (D)   6,464.6
> (E)   46,464

Solution: First multiply .20202 by 10^5. Just move the decimal point 5 places to the right. You get 20,202. (Use your calculator if you want.) Now you're going to subtract that from 66,666—but estimate it before you continue. Looks to be around 40,000 or so, doesn't it? So pick (E) and go on.

There are two advantages to solving the problem this way. First, you avoid having to do the last step of the problem and gain yourself some time. Second, you avoid even the possibility of making a careless mistake in that last step.

We know you can subtract. That's not the issue. On a timed test, with a lot of pressure on you, the fewer steps you have to do, the better off you are.

This is a fabulous piece of news—it means that you should use your eyes to estimate distances and angles, instead of jumping immediately to formulas and equations. You aren't allowed to bring a ruler or a protractor into the test. But you can often tell if one line is longer than another, or if the shaded part of a circle is larger than the unshaded part, just by estimating. That should allow you to eliminate at least a couple of answers, maybe more.

Is this a sleazy technique? Are we telling you to take the easy way out? No and yes. ETS, the company that writes the SAT, doesn't mind if you use your common sense. Neither do we. And as for the easy way out...yes, that's exactly what you're training yourself to look for.

Estimating is not totally foreign to you. Think of geometry problems you encounter in real life—parking a car, packing a box, even shooting a basketball. We guess you don't take out a pad and pencil and start calculating to solve any of these problems. You estimate them, and see what happens.

Same deal on the SAT.

For example:

What fractional part of the square is shaded?

(A) $\dfrac{1}{4}$

(B) $\dfrac{3}{10}$

(C) $\dfrac{1}{2}$

(D) $\dfrac{7}{12}$

(E) $\dfrac{15}{16}$

Solution: Just look at it. How much looks shaded? A little? No, so cross out (A) and (B). Most of it? No, so cross out (E). That leaves you with two answer choices, which isn't bad, since you haven't done any math. If you get stuck here, guess. Or count up how many shaded squares there are, and put that over the total number of squares. So the fractional part is $\dfrac{8}{16}$, or $\dfrac{1}{2}$.

The answer is (C).

QUICK QUIZ #3

EASY

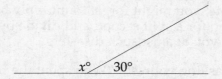

$x°$ $30°$

4. Which of the following is equal to 3x?

(A) 50
(B) 120
(C) 150
(D) 360
(E) 450

MEDIUM

13. Dan, Laura, and Jane went grocery shopping. Dan spent three times as much as Laura and half as much as Jane. If they spent a total of $50 on groceries, how much did Jane spend?

(A) $15
(B) $20
(C) $25
(D) $30
(E) $45

HARD

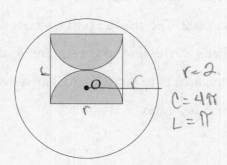

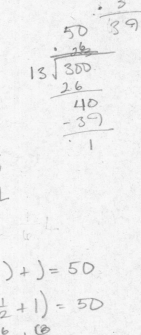

17. In the circle above with center O, the radius of the circle is equal to the length of a side of the square. If the shaded region represents two semicircles inscribed in the square, the ratio of the area of the shaded region to the area of the circle is

(A) 1:16
(B) 1:8
(C) 1:4
(D) 1:2
(E) 2:3

Answers and Explanations: Quick Quiz #3

4. **E** Angle x is pretty big, isn't it? So $3x$ is really, really big. Cross out (A), (B), and (C). Now work it out. $x + 30 = 180$, so $x = 150$. And $3x = 450$. If you fail to estimate, you might forget to multiply by 3 and pick (C). You might fall asleep for a split second and divide by 3 and pick (A). Estimating protects you against such disasters.

13. **D** You might start by asking yourself, "Who spent the most money?" Since Jane spent twice as much as Dan, and Dan spent three times as much as Laura, Jane spent the most. You can definitely eliminate A; it's too small an amount for Jane to have spent. Now Plug In the answer choices. Begin with (C) or (D), since (A) is out. Which is the easier number to cut in half?

	J	D	L
(D)	30	15	5

$30 + $15 + $5 = $50, so (D) is your answer.

17. **C** Look at the figure. How much of it looks shaded? Less than half? Sure. Cross out (D) and (E). If you're good at estimating, maybe you can cross out A as well. (Try drawing more semi-circles in the big circle and see how many will fit.) Now let's figure it out, using our good friend plugging in: Let the radius = 2. So the area is 4π. If the radius = 2, the side of the square is 2. The shaded part consists of 2 semi-circles, each with a radius that's $\frac{1}{2}$ the side of the square, so the radius of the small circle is 1, and the area is π. Put the small area over the big area and you get $\frac{\pi}{4\pi} = \frac{1}{4}$, which is a ratio of 1:4.

Tips for Estimating Happiness

- With geometry, especially on hard questions, the answer choices need to be translated into numbers that you can work with.

- Translate π to a bit more than 3; $\sqrt{2}$ is 1.4; $\sqrt{3}$ is 1.7.

- Practice estimating *a lot*, even if you're going to work out the problem—and notice how your estimates improve.

- The farther apart the answer choices, the bigger the opportunity for eliminating answers by estimating.

- If the figure is NOT drawn to scale, redraw it if you can, using whatever measurements are provided. Then go ahead and estimate. If you can't redraw it, don't estimate.

- If two things look about equal, you can't assume that they're *exactly* equal.

- Trust what your eyes tell you.

How to Apply These Techniques

To study efficiently for the SAT, you must:

- Practice plugging in. Plug in whenever and wherever you can.

- Analyze your work so that you can avoid making the same mistakes over and over.

- Do the problems in this book as though you are taking the real thing—practice with the same focus and intensity you will need on the actual SAT.

Arithmetic

Much of this chapter will be review, but study it well. Even though the SAT tests very basic mathematical concepts, these concepts are tested in very particular ways. To do well on the SAT requires that you know these definitions backward and forward.

After each section of review is a Quick Quiz with a variety of questions: easy, medium, and hard. If you get all of them right, you're in very good shape. And keep in mind: You could leave *all* the hard questions blank and still get a good score. So make sure you're getting the easy and medium ones right first.

DEFINITIONS

consecutive	numbers in order (1, 2, 3, etc.)
denominator	the bottom number of a fraction
difference	what you get when you subtract one number from another
digit	a number from 0 to 9. For example, 376 is a three-digit number.
distinct	different (i.e., the distinct factors of 4 are 1, 4, and 2—not 1, 4, 2, and 2)
even	a number evenly divisible by 2 (0 is even)
factor	same meaning as "division": a smaller number that goes into your number (example: 2 is a factor of 8)
multiple	a bigger number that your number goes into (example: 8 is a multiple of 2)
numerator	the top number of a fraction
odd	a number not evenly divisible by 2
PEMDAS	you won't see that written on the test—it's a handy acronym for the order of operations: Parentheses, Exponents, Multiplication, Division, Addition, Subtraction. Learn it, live it.
places	in 234.167, 2 is the hundreds place, 3 is the tens place, 4 is the ones or units digit, 1 is the tenths place, 6 is the hundredths place, and 7 is the thousandths place.
prime	a number divisible evenly only by itself and 1. The first five primes are 2, 3, 5, 7, and 11. (Note: 1 is *not* prime.)
product	what you get when you multiply two numbers together
quotient	what you get after dividing one number into another
reciprocal	whatever you multiply a number by to get 1 (i.e., the reciprocal of $\frac{1}{2}$ is $\frac{2}{1}$. The reciprocal of 6 is $\frac{1}{6}$.)
remainder	what's left over if a division problem doesn't work out evenly
sum	what you get when you add together two numbers

QUICK QUIZ #1

EASY

1. What is the greatest common prime factor of 32 and 28?

   (A) 1
   (B) 2
   (C) 3
   (D) 4
   (E) 7

MEDIUM

9. If x is a positive integer greater than 1, and $x(x + 4)$ is odd, then x must be

   (A) even
   (B) odd
   (C) prime
   (D) a factor of 8
   (E) divisible by 8

   $2(6) = 12$
   $3(7) = 21$
   $9(13) = 117$

HARD

20. The units digit of 2^{33} is how much less than the hundredths digit of $\dfrac{567}{1000}$?

    (A) 1
    (B) 2
    (C) 3
    (D) 4
    (E) 5

    2

    6

Answers and Explanations: Quick Quiz #1

1. **B** Plug in the answer choices. Why bother thinking up the answer yourself when they give you five choices? Since the question asks for the greatest common *prime* factor, you can cross out anything that isn't prime—get rid of (A) and (D). Now start with (E), because it's the greatest answer choice. Does 7 go into 32? No. Cross out (E). (C): Does 3 go into 28? No, cross out (C). That leaves us with (B). Does 2 go into 32 and 28? Yep.

9. **B** Plug in your own number for x. If x has to be a positive integer greater than 1, try $x = 2$. But $2(2 + 4)$ isn't odd. So try $x = 3$. $3(3 + 4) = 21$, which works. Now you can cross out everything but (B) and (C). Try an odd number that isn't prime, say $x = 9$. $9(9 + 4) = 117$, which is odd. So cross out (C).

20. **D** The units digit of any number has a pattern as the exponent goes up.

    $2^1 = 2$. $2^2 = 4$. $2^3 = 8$. $2^4 = 16$. $2^5 = 32$. $2^6 = 64$. See the pattern? The units digit of 2^x goes in a pattern of 2, 4, 8, 16, and then repeats forever, all the way to 2^{33} and beyond. So divide the number of elements in the pattern, which is 4, into 33. That gives you 8 with a remainder of 1. That means the pattern fully repeats 8 times, and then starts the pattern again with the first number. So the units' digit of 2^{33} is 2.

    To figure out the hundredths digit of $\dfrac{567}{1000}$, divide it on your calculator. You should get 0.567, which makes 6 the hundredths digit. 2 is 4 less than 6, so the answer is (D). (When we call these hard questions, we aren't kidding.)

DIVISIBILITY

On the SAT, **divisible** means divisible *evenly*, with no remainder. This means that 16 is divisible by 4, but 18 is *not* divisible by 4. To figure out whether one number is divisible by another, use your calculator.

Factoring shows up on the SAT all over the place. That's okay, it's easy.

To find all of the factors of a number, factor in pairs. Start with 1 and make a list of all the pairs that multiply together to equal the original number:

What are the factors of 36?

1, 36

2, 18

3, 12

4, 9

6, 6

To find the **prime factors** of a number, simply find all the factors as shown above, and then select only those that are also prime numbers.

3 2

QUICK QUIZ #2

EASY

n=1   n=2

2. Which of the following could be a factor of
   $n(n + 1)$, if n is a positive integer less than 3?

   (A) 3   *1(1+1) = 2*
   (B) 4   *2(3) = 6*
   (C) 5
   (D) 8
   (E) 9

MEDIUM

10. If Darlene divided 210 chocolate kisses into
    bags containing the same number of kisses,
    each of the following could be the number of
    kisses per bag EXCEPT

    (A) 35
    (B) 21
    (C) 20
    (D) 15
    (E) 14

HARD

19. If $p = 2^2 \cdot 3^2 \cdot 7$, and y is a positive integer,

    what is the greatest number of values for y such

    that $\dfrac{p}{18y}$ is an integer?

    (A) 2
    (B) 3
    (C) 4
    (D) 5
    (E) 6

$$\frac{2^2 \cdot 3^2 \cdot 7}{18y} = \frac{252}{18y}$$

$$\frac{14}{y} \quad | \; 2714$$

Answers and Explanations: Quick Quiz #2

2. **A** Plug in. If $n = 1$, $1(1 + 1) = 2$. None of the answers are factors of 2. If $n = 2$, $2(2+1) = 6$. 3 is a factor of 6, so the answer is (A).

10. **C** You could use your calculator and divide each answer into 210, then pick the one that doesn't go evenly. Or you could factor 210 as $7 \times 5 \times 3 \times 2$. Now factor the answers. (A): 7×5, which goes in, so cross it out. (B): 7×3. Cross it out. (C): $2 \times 2 \times 5$. That doesn't go in because there's only one factor of 2 in 210.

19. **C** Let's write this a slightly different way: $\dfrac{2 \times 2 \times 3 \times 3 \times 7}{2 \times 3 \times 3y}$. Cancel and you get $\dfrac{14}{y}$. How many different numbers can y be if $\dfrac{14}{y}$ is an integer? $y = 1, 2, 7,$ or 14. Four values.

FRACTIONS

To add fractions, get a common denominator and then add across the top:

$$\frac{1}{2} + \frac{2}{3} = \frac{3}{6} + \frac{4}{6} = \frac{7}{6}$$

To subtract fractions, it's the same deal, but subtract across the top:

$$\frac{3}{4} - \frac{1}{3} = \frac{9}{12} - \frac{4}{12} = \frac{5}{12}$$

To multiply fractions, cancel if you can, then multiply across, top and bottom:

$$\frac{1}{2} \cdot \frac{3}{5} = \frac{3}{10} \qquad\qquad \frac{2}{7} \cdot \frac{\overset{2}{\cancel{14}}}{\underset{1}{9}} = \frac{4}{19}$$

To divide fractions, flip the second one, then multiply across, top and bottom:

$$\frac{2}{3} \div \frac{1}{2} = \frac{2}{3} \cdot \frac{2}{1} = \frac{4}{3}$$

To see which of the two fractions is bigger, cross-multiply from bottom to top. The side with the bigger product is the bigger fraction.

$$55 \nwarrow \frac{5}{7} \times \frac{8}{11} \nearrow 56$$

56 is bigger than 55, so $\dfrac{8}{11}$ is bigger.

QUICK QUIZ #3

EASY

3. Which of the following is greatest?

   (A) $\frac{3}{5} \times \frac{5}{3} =$ $\frac{15}{15} = 1$

   (B) $\frac{3}{5} \div \frac{5}{3} =$ $\frac{9}{25}$

   (C) $\frac{3}{5} + \frac{3}{5} =$ $\frac{6}{5}$

   (D) $\frac{5}{3} - \frac{3}{5} =$ $\frac{16}{15}$

   (E) $\frac{5}{3} \div \frac{3}{5} =$ $\frac{25}{9}$

MEDIUM

13. Boris ate $\frac{1}{2}$ a pizza on Monday and $\frac{2}{3}$ of the remainder on Tuesday. What fractional part of the pizza was left?

    (A) $\frac{3}{5}$

    (B) $\frac{1}{3}$ $\frac{1}{2}$ $\frac{2}{3}$ $\frac{2}{6} =$

    (C) $\frac{1}{4}$

    (D) $\frac{1}{6}$

    (E) $\frac{1}{12}$

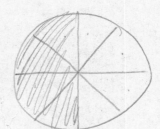

20. At a track meet, $\frac{2}{5}$ of the first-place finishers attended Southport High School, and $\frac{1}{2}$ of them were girls. If $\frac{2}{9}$ of the first-place finishers who did NOT attend Southport High School were girls, what fractional part of the total number of first-place finishers were boys?

(A) $\frac{1}{9}$

(B) $\frac{2}{15}$

(C) $\frac{7}{18}$

(D) $\frac{3}{5}$

(E) $\frac{2}{3}$

ANSWERS AND EXPLANATIONS: QUICK QUIZ #3

3. **E** You can do some estimating here, but be careful—remember that when you divide by a fraction, you're really multiplying by the reciprocal. (E) is $\frac{5}{3} \div \frac{3}{5}$, which is $\frac{5}{3} \times \frac{5}{3} = \frac{25}{9}$. (A): 1. (B): $\frac{9}{25}$. (C): $\frac{6}{5}$. (D): $\frac{16}{25}$. If you had trouble figuring out any of those, go back to the fraction review.

13. **D** Let's plug in and say that Boris's pizza had 6 slices. If he ate $\frac{1}{2}$, then he ate 3 slices and had 3 slices left. If he then ate $\frac{2}{3}$ of 3, he ate 2 slices and had 1 slice left. So the final fractional part is 1, over the original whole of 6, or $\frac{1}{6}$. How did we know to plug in 6? We looked at the denominators of the fractions we were going to have to work with and picked a number that they would go into evenly. If you pick a bad number, don't worry, just pick a new one.

20. **E** Let's plug in. The total number of first-place finishers was 30. We can find the number who were from Southport by taking $\frac{2}{5}$ of 30 = 12. That leaves 18 who did not go to Southport High School. If half the 12 Southport runners were girls, that means 6 were girls and 6 were boys. If $\frac{2}{9}$ of the non-Southport runners were girls, then $\frac{2}{9}$ of 18 = 4 girls, which leaves 14 boys. That means a total of 14 + 6 = 20 boys, out of a total of 30, or $\frac{20}{30} = \frac{2}{3}$. You will be happier if you make a tree chart:

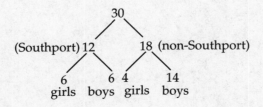

DECIMALS

To add, subtract, multiply, or divide decimals, use your calculator. Remember to check each number as you punch it in, and be extra careful with the decimal point.

To convert a fraction to a decimal, use your calculator to divide the numerator by the denominator:

$$\frac{1}{2} = 1 \div 2 = .5 \qquad \frac{5}{8} = 5 \div 8 = .625 \qquad \frac{4}{3} = 1.333$$

To convert a decimal to a fraction, count up the number of digits to the right of the decimal point and put that many zeros in your denominator:

$$0.2 = \frac{2}{10} \qquad .314 = \frac{314}{1000} \qquad 2.23 = \frac{223}{100}$$

QUICK QUIZ #4

EASY

1. If $0.2p = 4$, then $4p =$

   (A) 0.2
   (B) 2
   (C) 8
   (D) 40
   (E) 80

   [handwritten: $0.2p = 4$, $p = 4/.02$]

MEDIUM

10. For positive integers y and z, if $z^2 = y^3$ and $y^2 = 16$, then $\frac{y}{z} =$

    (A) 0.8
    (B) 0.5
    (C) 0.4
    (D) 0.2
    (E) 2

    [handwritten: $y = 4$, $z = 8$, $\frac{4}{8}$]

HARD

19. $\dfrac{\frac{ad}{bc}}{\frac{ac}{bd}} =$

    [handwritten: $\frac{ad}{bc} \cdot \frac{bd}{ac}$, $\frac{d^2}{c^2}$]

    (A) 1
    (B) a^2c^2
    (C) $\dfrac{a^2}{b^2}$
    (D) $\dfrac{d^2}{c^2}$
    (E) b^2d^2

Answers and Explanations: Quick Quiz #4

1. **E** If $0.2p = 4$, then $p = 20$, and $4p = 80$.
10. **B** If $y^2 = 16$, then $y = 4$. If $z^2 = y^3$, then $z^2 = 64$ and $z = 8$.

   So $\dfrac{y}{z} = \dfrac{4}{8} = \dfrac{1}{2} = 0.5$.

19. **D** Remember that to divide fractions you flip the denominator and multiply. (Dividing is the same as multiplying by the reciprocal.)

   So $\dfrac{\frac{ad}{bc}}{\frac{ac}{bd}} = \dfrac{ad}{bc} \bullet \dfrac{bd}{ac} = \dfrac{adbd^2}{abc^2} = \dfrac{d^2}{c^2}$.

PERCENTAGES

For some reason, many people get hung up on percents, probably because they are trying to remember a series of operations rather than using their common sense.

A percentage is simply a fractional part—50% of something is one-half of something, and 47% is a little less than half. It is very helpful to approximate percents in this way, and not to think of them as abstract, meaningless numbers. 3.34% is very little of something, 0.0012% a tiny part of something, and 105% a little more than the whole.

Keep in mind that since percents are an expression of the fractional part, they do not represent actual numbers. If, for example, you're a salesperson, and you earn a 15% commission on what you sell, you'll get a lot richer selling Rolls-Royces than you will selling doughnuts. Even thousands of doughnuts. All examples of 15% are not created equal, unless they are 15% of the same number.

Now for the nitty-gritty:

To convert a percent to a decimal, move the decimal point two spaces to the left:

   50% = .5   4% = .04   .03% = .0003   112% = 1.12

To convert a decimal to a percent, move the decimal point two spaces to the right:

   .5 = 50%   .66 = 66%   .01 = 1%   4 = 400%

To convert a percent to a fraction, put the number over 100:

   $50\% = \dfrac{50}{100}$ $4\% = \dfrac{4}{100}$ $106\% = \dfrac{106}{100}$ $x = \dfrac{x}{100}$

To get a percent of a number, multiply by the decimal. So to get 22% of 50, first change the percentage to a decimal by moving the decimal point two places to the left = .22. Then multiply on your calculator.

The second way to get a percent of a number is to transform your sentence into an equation. This is easier than it sounds. Convert the percent to a fraction and substitute × for *of*, = for *is*, and x for *what*.

What is 50% of 16?

This question transforms to $x = \dfrac{50}{100} \times 16$.

This method is particularly useful for complicated percents:

What is 10% of 40% of 22?

This question transforms to $x = \dfrac{10}{100} \times \dfrac{40}{100} \times 22$.

To calculate what percent one number is of another number, use the transformation method, substituting $\dfrac{x}{100}$ for *what percent*.

What percent of 16 is 8?

This question transforms to $\dfrac{x}{100} \times 16 = 8$.

$8 = \dfrac{x}{100} \cdot 16$

8 is what percent of 16?

This question transforms to $8 = \dfrac{x}{100} \times 16$.

Notice that even though these equations look a little different, they will produce the same answer.

Another way: Since figuring out what percentage one number is of another number is nothing more than figuring out the fractional part, you can solve these questions by setting up a proportion.

8 is what percent of 16?

This question can be written as $\dfrac{8}{16} = \dfrac{x}{100}$.

What percent of 30 is 6?

This question can be written as $\dfrac{6}{30} = \dfrac{x}{100}$.

What we're doing here is putting the part over the whole. Note that the part is usually the smaller number, but not always. The number that follows *of* will be the whole, and the number that comes right before or after *is* will be the part.

QUICK QUIZ #5

EASY

3. If 20% of p is 10, then 10% of p is

(A) 2
(B) 4
(C) 5
(D) 8
(E) 14

[handwritten: $.2p = 10$, $p = 10/.2$, $(.1 \times \frac{10}{.20})$]

MEDIUM

11. Mabel agreed to pay the tax and tip for dinner at a restaurant with her four friends. Each of the friends paid an equal part of the cost of the dinner, which was $96. If the tax and tip together were 20% of the cost of the meal, Mabel paid how much less than any one of her friends?

[handwritten: 96]

(A) $2.40
(B) $4.80
(C) $9.20
(D) $19.20
(E) $24.00

[handwritten: 19.2, 24]

HARD

18. If 200% of 40% of x is equal to 40% of y, then x is what percent of y?

(A) 10%
(B) 20%
(C) 30%
(D) 50%
(E) 80%

[handwritten: $2. : 4. \times x = .4y$, $.8x = .4y$, $x = .5y$]

Answers and Explanations: Quick Quiz #5

3. **C** 10% is half of 20%, and half of 10 is 5. That way we don't have to worry about p. To figure p, transform the sentence: $\frac{20}{100} \times p = 10$. $\frac{p}{5} = 10$, and $p = 50$. Now do the next step: $0.1 \times 50 = 5$.

11. **B** First calculate what each friend paid: $96 \div 4 = \$24$. Now do the percentage: $0.20 \times 96 = \$19.20$. Subtract the second number from the first. If you noticed that each of the four friends paid 25%, and Mabel paid 20%, you could take a fast shortcut by taking the difference, or 5% of 96. [If you picked (D) or (E), you should reread the question before picking your final answer.]

18. **D** Plug in $100 = x$. 40% of 100 is 40, and 200% of 40 is $2 \times 40 = 80$. Now our question says that 80 is 40% of y, so $y = 200$. $(80 = 0.4y)$ The question asks "x is what percent of y?", which you can write out as $100 = \frac{p}{100} \times 200$. Or you can set up a proportion: $\frac{p}{100} = \frac{100}{200}$. Or you can simply realize that 100 is half of 200, which is 50%.

More on Percentages

To calculate percent increase or decrease, use the following formula:

$$\text{percent increase or decrease} = \frac{\text{difference}}{\text{original amount}} = \frac{x}{100}$$

For instance, if a \$40 book was reduced to \$35, the difference in price is \$5. Therefore, the percent decrease is equal to $\frac{5}{40}$, which is the same as $\frac{1}{8}$ or 12.5.

QUICK QUIZ #6

MEDIUM

14. A store owner buys a pound of grapes for 80 cents and sells it for a dollar. What percent of the selling price of grapes is the store owner's profit?

    (A) 10%
    (B) 20%
    (C) 25%
    (D) 40%
    (E) 80%

HARD

17. On the first test of the semester, Barbara scored a 60. On the last test of the semester, Barbara scored a 75. By what percent did Barbara's score improve?

    (A) 12%
    (B) 15%
    (C) 18%
    (D) 20%
    (E) 25%

20. Randy's chain of used car dealerships sold 16,400 cars in 1998. If the chain sold 15,744 cars in 1999, by what percent did the number of cars sold decrease?

    (A) 1%
    (B) 4%
    (C) 11%
    (D) 40%
    (E) 65%

14. **B** First determine the store owner's profit. Change everything to cents so that you're only working with one unit: $100 - 80 = 20$. Now translate the question into math terms: $\dfrac{x}{100} \bullet 100 = 20$.

17. **E** Find the difference: $75 - 60 = 15$. Put this difference (15) over the lower number: $\dfrac{15}{60}$. Reduce the fraction to $\dfrac{1}{4}$, which is 25%. Or divide it on your calculator, which will give you 0.25. Convert it to a percentage by moving the decimal two places to the right.

20. **B** Get the difference: $16{,}400 - 15{,}744 = 656$. Put 656 over the higher number: $\dfrac{656}{16{,}400} = 0.04 = 4\%$. Use your calculator.

> **TIP:**
>
> **Estimating is always a good idea when you're doing a percentage question—a lot of the time there are silly answers that you can cross out before you do any math at all.**

RATIOS

A ratio is like a percentage—it tells you how much you have of one thing compared to how much you have of another thing. For example, if you have hats and T-shirts in a ratio of 2:3, then for every two hats, you have three T-shirts. What we don't know is the actual number of each. It could be two hats and three T-shirts. Or it could be four hats and six T-shirts. Or 20 hats and 30 T-shirts.

A ratio describes a relationship, not a total number.

To figure the actual numbers in a ratio, add the numbers in the ratio and divide into the total. Take that number and multiply by both parts.

> John has red marbles and blue marbles in a ratio of 1:2. If he has a total of 24 marbles, how many red and blue marbles does he have?

Add the numbers in the ratio: $1 + 2 = 3$. Now divide 3 into 24 and get 8. Multiply that number by the parts in the ratio by that number: $8 \times 1 = 8$, and $8 \times 2 = 16$. So there are 8 red marbles and 16 blue marbles.

To check your answer, add the actual parts together. They should add up to the original total. 8 + 16 = 24, so the answer is correct.

Note that the two actual numbers are really the same ratio, but unreduced. All we've done is multiply both parts of 1:2 by 8 to get 8:16.

> **TIP**
>
> **Don't get the order of the ratio mixed up—if the problem says red marbles and blue marbles in a ratio of 1:2, the first number represents the red marbles and the second number represents the blue marbles.**

QUICK QUIZ #7

MEDIUM

12. If $\dfrac{x}{y} = \dfrac{4}{3}$ and $\dfrac{x}{k} = \dfrac{1}{2}$, then $\dfrac{k}{y} =$

(A) $\dfrac{1}{6}$

(B) $\dfrac{3}{8}$

(C) $\dfrac{2}{3}$

(D) $\dfrac{3}{2}$

(E) $\dfrac{8}{3}$

$3x = 4y \qquad \dfrac{3}{4}x = y$

$2x = 1k \qquad 2x = k$

$\dfrac{2x}{\frac{3}{4}x} = \dfrac{2x \cdot 4}{3x} = \dfrac{8}{3}$

16. The junior class at Mooreland High is composed of boys and girls in a ratio of 5:1. All of the following could be the number of students in the junior class EXCEPT

(A) 66
(B) 84
(C) 114
(D) 138
(E) 178

HARD

20. Forty gallons of a certain mixture is made up of 3 parts water and 5 parts Liquid X. If the mixture must be changed in order to be 75% Liquid X, how many gallons of Liquid X must be added to the original mixture?

(A) 15
(B) 20
(C) 35
(D) 50
(E) 60

$\begin{array}{cc} W & X \\ 3 : 5 & \qquad 15:25 \end{array}$

$W = 37.5\%$

$X = 62.5\%$ $\qquad 15:60$

12. **E** Since $x = 4$ in one ratio and $x = 1$ in the other, we can't compare them.

First we have to make them equal. If you multiply the second ratio by $\frac{4}{4}$, you get $\frac{4}{4}$. (Notice that if you multiply all parts of the ratio by the same number, it doesn't change. It just takes an unreduced form.)

Now the x's are the same in both ratios, so you can compare them, and $\frac{k}{y} = \frac{8}{3}$. You could also plug in, which would work at least as well.

16. **E** If the ratio is 5:1, we can add the parts and get 6 students. Therefore the number of students in the class must be a multiple of 6. All of the choices are multiples of 6 except (E).

20. **B** First figure out how much actual water and Liquid X you have. Add the parts of the ratio, $3 + 5 = 8$, and divide that sum into the total. $40 \div 8 = 5$. Now multiply the ratio by that quotient, making the ratio 15:25. (Same ratio, but representing actual gallons.) Now let's plug in the answer choices. Take (B): If we add 20 gallons of Liquid X, we get 15:45. That's 45 gallons of X out of a total of 60 gallons, which is 75%.

PROPORTIONS

To set up a proportion, match categories on top and bottom. For example:

If 10 nails cost 4 cents, how much do 50 nails cost?

$$\text{(nails)} \quad \frac{10}{4} = \frac{50}{x} \quad \text{(cents)}$$

$$10x = 200, \text{ so } x = 20 \text{ cents}$$

The great thing about proportions is that it doesn't matter which is on top—if you match nails to nails and cents to cents (or whatever), you'll get the right answer. Be consistent.

To solve an **inverse variation** problem, use the following set-up.

$$x_1y_1 = x_2y_2$$

If the value of x is inversely proportional to the value of y and $y = 4$ when $x = 15$, what is the value of x when y is 12?

$$x(12) = (15)(4)$$
$$x = 5$$

To solve rate problems, set up a proportion:

If Bonzo rode his unicycle 30 miles in 5 hours, how long would it take him to ride 12 miles at the same rate?

$$\text{(miles)} \quad \frac{30}{5} = \frac{12}{x} \quad \text{(hours)}$$

$$30x = 60$$

$$x = 2 \text{ hours}$$

QUICK QUIZ #8

EASY

2. Laura can solve 6 math questions in 12 minutes. Working at the same rate, how many minutes would it take Laura to solve 5 math questions?

    (A) 6
    (B) 8
    (C) 9
    (D) 10
    (E) 11

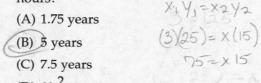

MEDIUM

8. The length of time in hours that a certain battery will last is inversely proportional to the length of time in years that the battery spends in storage. If the battery spends 3 years in storage, it will last 25 hours, so how long must the battery have been in storage if it will last 15 hours?

    (A) 1.75 years

    (B) 5 years

    (C) 7.5 years

    (D) $41\frac{2}{3}$ years

    (E) 75 years

HARD

16. A factory produced 15 trucks of the same model. If the trucks had a combined weight of $34\frac{1}{2}$ tons, how much, in pounds, did one of the trucks weigh? (One ton = 2000 pounds)

    (A) 460
    (B) 2200
    (C) 4500
    (D) 4600
    (E) 5400

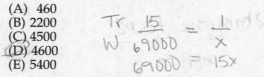

ANSWERS AND EXPLANATION: QUICK QUIZ #8

2. **D** $\frac{6}{12} = \frac{5}{x}$. Cross-multiply to get $6x = 10$.

8. **B** To do this problem, it is important to know the formula for inverse variation: $x_1 y_1 = x_2 y_2$. In this case, the x_1 is 3 years, y_1 is 25 hours, and y_2 is 15 hours. So set up the equation as follows: $3 \times 25 = x_2 \times 15$. $\frac{75}{15} = x_2 = 5$ years.

16. **D** You can do this two ways: You can convert from tons to pounds first or do it later. If you do it first, multiply 34.5×2000. That gives you 69,000. Your proportion should look like this: $\frac{15}{69,000} = \frac{1}{x}$. So $15x = 69,000$, and $x = 4600$. Or you can divide 15 into 34.5, which gives you 2.3 tons per truck. Then multiply 2.3 times 2000.

AVERAGES

You already know how to figure out an average. You can figure out your GPA, right?

To get the average (arithmetic mean) of a set of numbers, add them up, then divide by the number of things in the set:

What's the average of 3, 5, and 10? $3 + 5 + 10 = 18$ and $18 \div 3 = 6$.

Most of the time on the SAT you are not given a set of numbers and asked for the average—they want to make their questions a little harder than that. There are three elements at work here: the sum of the numbers, the number of things in the set, and the average. To get any of these elements, you need to know the other two.

The easy way to remember these relationships is by memorizing the "Average Pie."

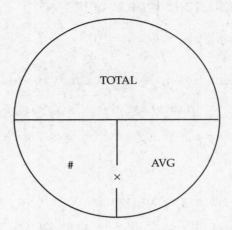

If you want to find any one element, cover it up, and what remains is the formula for finding it.

- The sum divided by the number of things = the average.

- The sum divided by the average = the number of things.

- The average multiplied by the number of things = the sum.

To solve an average problem, put whatever elements you are given into the average pie, and solve for the remaining element. The problem will always give you two parts out of the three, which will enable you to solve for the third.

QUICK QUIZ #9

EASY

6. The average of 3 numbers is 22, and the smallest of these numbers is 2. If the other two numbers are equal, each of them is

(A) 22
(B) 30
(C) 32
(D) 40
(E) 64

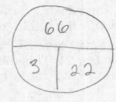

$64 = x + x$

MEDIUM

12. Caroline scored 85, 88, and 89 on three of her four history tests. If her average score for all tests was 90, what did she score on her fourth test?

(A) 89
(B) 90
(C) 93
(D) 96
(E) 98

$4 \times 90 = 85 + 88 + 89 + x$
$360 = 262 + x$
$x = 98$

HARD

14. The average of 8, 13, x, and y is 6. The average of 15, 9, x, and x is 8. What is the value of y?

(A) −1
(B) 0
(C) 4
(D) 6
(E) 8

$8, 13, x, y = 6$

$15, 9, x, x \sqrt{8}$

$x = 4$

$8, 13, 4, y = 6$

$x + y = 5$

$4 + y = 5$

$-1 = y$

$x = 4$

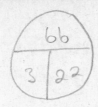

ANSWERS AND EXPLANATIONS: QUICK QUIZ #9

6. **C** If the average of 3 numbers is 22, then their sum is 3×22 or 66. Take away the 2 and you've got 64 left. If the other two numbers are equal, divide 64 by 2 = 32.

12. **E** We know that Caroline's final average was 90 on 4 tests. Therefore we can use the average pie to figure out the total number of points she had on those four tests, by multiplying $90 \times 4 = 360$. We also know her scores on the first three tests, so if we subtract $360 - 85 - 88 - 89$, we get 98 points, which is the total score she must have gotten on her fourth test.

14. **A** Since the average of 8, 13, x, and y is 6, we know that their total must be equal to 6×4 or 24. This means that $8 + 13 + x + y = 24$. If we subtract the 8 and the 13, we can solve that $x + y = 3$. We also know that the average of 15, 9, x, and x is 8, so their total must be equal to 32. $15 + 9 + x + x = 32$, so $x + x$ must equal 8, and $x = 4$. Since we know from earlier that $x + y = 3$, we can solve that $y = -1$.

MEDIAN, MODE, SET, INTERSECTION, AND UNION

Each of these terms involves finding a value or values in **sets** of numbers. A **set** is just a fancy term for a list of numbers.

To find the median, first put the group of numbers in ascending order. If the group has an odd number of elements, the median is the middle number.

    set: 1, 4, 9, 18, 54   median: 9
    set: 2, 4, 4, 4, 5   median: 4

If the group has an even number of elements, the median is *the average (arithmetic mean) of* the two middle numbers.

    set: 3, 15, 17, 74   median: 16
    set: 1, 6, 7, 8   median: 6.5

To find the mode, just look to see which number in the group appears the most often.

    set: 1, 1, 3, 5, 3, 4, 22, 3, 6   mode: 3
    set: 2, 5, 9, 11, 11, 15, 22   mode: 11

To find the intersection, list all the elements common to both sets.

    set: 2, 5, 8, 9, 12, 17

    set: 5, 9, 17, 25, 43   intersection: 5, 9, 17

The symbol for intersection is ∩.

To find the union, list all of the elements in each set.

    set: 2, 11, 13, 19, 33, 41

    set: 4, 8, 18, 19, 39, 75   union: 2, 4, 8, 11, 13, 18, 19, 33, 39, 41, 75

The symbol for union is ∪. Note that even though the number 19 appears in both sets, it is only listed once for purposes of finding the union.

QUICK QUIZ #10

EASY

Set Q: {10, 2, 3, 5, 1, 7, 5, 2}

6. If the smallest and largest numbers in Set Q are removed, what is the median of Set Q?

   (A) 3.5

   (B) 4

   (C) 5

   (D) 6

   (E) 7

MEDIUM

A: {3,6,8,9,11,15}

B: {1,4,6,8,13,17,22}

C: {2,5,6,9,17,19}

12. Sets A, B, and C are shown above. What is the set that is the result of $A \cup (B \cap C)$?

   (A) {3,6,6,8,9,11,15,17}

   (B) {3,6,8,9,11,15,17}

   (C) {6}

   (D) {6,17}

   (E) {1,2,3,4,11,13,15,22}

Hard

August Temperature Readings in Plainville

Temperature Range (in degrees)	Frequency (in days)
66–70	3
71–75	6
76–80	5
81–85	8
86–90	7
91–95	2

15 - 19

18. The difference between the mode of the temperature ranges in August and the lowest recorded temperature falls within which of the following ranges?

(A) 11–15 degrees
(B) 13–17 degrees
(C) 15–17 degrees
(D) 15–19 degrees
(E) 19–22 degrees

Answers and Explanations: Quick Quiz #10

6. **B** Take out 10 and 1. Now write down the numbers in order: 2, 2, 3, 5, 5, 7. The middle of the list falls between 3 and 5, so the median is 4.

12. **B** First start with the sets inside the parentheses. The problem asks us to find the intersection of sets B and C. There are only two numbers that are common to both sets: {6, 17}. Now take the newly created set and find the union of it with set A. This should include all of the values either of the sets have, minus any repeats. So the final set should include all of the numbers in set A, with an added 17 from $B \cap C$. However, it should not contain two 6s, so (B) is the best answer.

18. **D** The mode is 81–85, since there are more days with temperatures in that range than any other. The lowest possible recorded temperature is 66, and to get the difference between that and the mode, we need to subtract 66 from 81 and from 85. That should give you 15 and 19.

STANDARD DEVIATION

Standard deviation is a tricky concept that shows up once in a while on the SAT. The key is to memorize the percentages found in a normal distribution (also known as a bell curve). Take a look at the following graph:

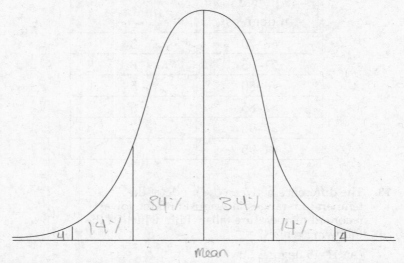

In a normal distribution, the **mean** of the set of numbers lies on the middle of the curve.

Standard deviation is a term used to describe how far from the mean a particular number in the set lies. You won't have to calculate the standard deviation; ETS will always provide it.

To either side of the mean are the values one standard deviation greater than the mean and one standard deviation smaller than the mean. These two brackets encompass 68% of the data—34% smaller than the mean and 34% larger than the mean.

Farther out are the percentiles for numbers two standard deviations from the mean. These brackets account for 28% of the data, with half of that (14%) again greater than the mean and the other half smaller than the mean.

The final 4% of the data lies three standard deviations from the mean. While this seems to be a strange concept, all it really means is that in a normal distribution, most of the data is clustered around the mean. A small part of the data lies a bit farther away from the mean, and only a tiny portion "deviates" enough from the mean to lie at the extreme edges of the graph.

QUICK QUIZ #11

$\dfrac{6x}{100} = 12.5$

EASY

3. Which of the following lists of numbers has the largest standard deviation?

   (A) 1,4,5,6   4 5.36 2.64
   (B) 5,5,5,5
   (C) 7,10,11,13   10.25 13.85 6.765
   (D) 6,9,15,20   12.5 16.75 8.25
   (E) 45,47,47,50   47.25 63.315 31.185

   has the largest range

MEDIUM

11. Ricardo currently has a C in chemistry, but if he scores at least two standard deviations above the mean on the final, he can raise his grade to a B. If the average student in his chemistry class gets 57 points out of a possible 85 on the final, and the standard deviation is 6 points, which of the following is a possible number of points on the final that will give Ricardo a B in chemistry?

    (A) 44
    (B) 50
    (C) 57
    (D) 68
    (E) 71

    $6 \cdot 2 = 12$ $57 + 12 = 69$
    $71 > 69$

HARD

20. Mrs. Thompson gave a math test that had 30 questions worth 1 point apiece. Mrs. Thompson doesn't give any partial credit on questions, and when she scored the test, she found her students got an average of 89%, with a standard deviation of 4%. If Katherine scored inside of 3 standard deviations for the test, how many possible percent scores could Katherine have had?

    (A) 5
    (B) 6
    (C) 7
    (D) 8
    (E) 9

    30
    92.56
    85.44

    $.04 \cdot 89 = 3.56 \times 4 = 10.68$
    $4 \cdot 3 = 12$
    $89 + 12 = 101$
    $89 - 12 = 77$
    77% - 100%

    77 80 83 87% 90%, 93% 97%

3. **D** In order to find a list of numbers that has the largest standard deviation, we need to look for a list that encompasses the largest range. The values in (D) range from 6 to 20, which is much larger than the range of any of the other answers.

11. **E** For Ricardo to raise his grade to a B, he must get at least two standard deviations above the average score. Since the standard deviation is 6, he needs 12 points or more than the average. The average score is 57 points, so Ricardo needs a score of 69 points or higher. Only (E) works.

20. **D** First check to see how high or low Katherine could have scored on the test to be inside three standard deviations. The range would give us anywhere between 77% and 101%, or really 100%, since we can't get higher than 100%. The next thing to look for is what the possible scores are: 100% is possible if you get all of the questions right. If Katherine misses one, 29 points out of 30 would give a 97%, which is another possible score. In fact, because of how the test is scored, possible scores happen every 3%. So the full list that is inside our standard deviation range is: 100%, 97%, 94%, 91%, 88%, 85%, 82%, 79%. That list has 8 possible scores, so the best answer is (D).

EXPONENTS

An exponent tells you how many times to multiply a number by itself. So x^3 is really shorthand for $x \cdot x \cdot x$. If you have a momentary lapse and can't remember the following rules, it may help to write out your problem the long way and work from there.

For exponents with the same base:

To multiply, add the exponents: $x^2 \cdot x^5 = x^{2+5} = x^7$

To divide, subtract the exponents: $x^6 \div x^3 = x^{6-3} = x^3$

To raise the power, multiply: $(x^4)^3 = x^{4 \cdot 3} = x^{12}$

You cannot add or subtract different exponents, so $x^6 + x^3$ is just $x^6 + x^3$. You can't reduce it.

For exponents with different bases:

The trick is to try to rewrite the numbers in terms of the same base. For example:

$$6^2 \times 12^4$$
becomes
$$(2 \times 3)^2 \times (2 \times 2 \times 3)^4$$

Now you can combine terms with the same base as above.

To deal with exponents and parentheses, remember that the exponent carries over to all parts within the parentheses:

$$2(3a^3)^2 = 2[(3^2)(a^6)] = 2(9a^6) = 18a^6$$

Keep in mind that 1 raised to any power is still just 1. ($1^{357} = 1$.)

Negative numbers with even exponents are positive; negative numbers with odd exponents are negative. Fractions with exponents get smaller, not bigger.

Rational exponents combine powers with roots. To simplify the following expression:

$$8^{\frac{2}{3}}$$

First we raise the base to the power of the numerator of the fraction. In this case, the numerator is two, so we'll square the base and get the following:

$$8^2 = 64$$

Now we'll deal with the denominator of the fraction. The denominator tells us what root to take the number to. In this case, the denominator is three, so we'll find the third root and end up with the following:

$$\sqrt[3]{64} = 4$$

QUICK QUIZ #12

EASY

1. If $(3x)^2 = 81$, then $x =$

   (A) 2
   (B) 3
   (C) 6
   (D) 9
   (E) 12

MEDIUM

16. If $a > 0$, $b < 1$, and $c < 0$, assuming $b \neq 0$, which of the following must be true?

    (A) abc is positive.

    (B) abc is negative.

    (C) a^2b^2c is positive.

    (D) ab^2c^2 is positive.

    (E) $a^3b^3c^3$ is negative.

HARD

18. $2a^{\frac{1}{3}}b^{\frac{2}{3}} =$

    (A) $\left(2\sqrt[3]{ab^2}\right)$

    (B) $\left(2\sqrt{ab^3}\right)$

    (C) $\left(3\sqrt[3]{ab^2}\right)$

    (D) $\left(2\sqrt[3]{a^2b^2}\right)$

    (E) $\left(2\sqrt{a^3b^2}\right)$

Answers and Explanations: Quick Quiz #12

1. **B** Square everything within the parentheses, so you get $3^2x^2 = 81$, or $9x^2 = 81$. Divide by 9 and you get $x^2 = 9$, and x could equal 3.

16. **D** Your life will be easier if you make a little chart showing the signs of each variable:

    $a +$

    $b\ ?$

    $c -$

    Now go to the answers. If we don't know the sign of b, we don't know the sign of choices (A), (B), or (E). In (C), a^2 is positive, b^2 will have to be positive no matter what the sign of b is, and c is negative. So the whole thing is negative. Our answer is (D).

18. **A** Since a and b have a common denominator, you know that you will find the cube root of ab: $\sqrt[3]{ab}$. Eliminate (B) and (E). Since the numerator of the exponent of a is 1 and of b is 2, you know you will raise a to the power of 1 and b to the power of 2. Eliminate (D). The 2 in the equation is being multiplied by a and b, so that will remain the same. Eliminate (C).

ROOTS

In the 1970s, it was a wildly popular mini-series. On the SAT, it's a type of question that gives a lot of people a big headache. Expect to see about one to four square root questions on your test.

A square root is just a backward exponent; in other words, the number under the $\sqrt{\ }$ is what you get when you raise a number to a power of 2.

$$\sqrt{4} = 2 \qquad\qquad \sqrt{36} = 6 \qquad\qquad \sqrt{1} = 1$$

To multiply or divide square roots, just multiply or divide as usual.

$$\sqrt{7} \bullet \sqrt{3} = \sqrt{21} \quad \sqrt{15} \div \sqrt{3} = \sqrt{5}$$

To add or subtract square roots, first make sure you have the same number under the $\sqrt{\ }$. Then add or subtract the number outside of the $\sqrt{\ }$.

$$5\sqrt{3} + 2\sqrt{3} = 7\sqrt{3} \qquad 6\sqrt{2} - \sqrt{2} = 5\sqrt{2}$$

Note that:

- A square root multiplied by itself is just that number without the $\sqrt{\ }$. $\left(\sqrt{3} \bullet \sqrt{3} = 3\right)$

- The square root of a fraction gets bigger. For example, $\sqrt{\dfrac{1}{4}} = \dfrac{1}{2}$.

- The square root of a number is always positive (on the SAT, anyway).

- The square root of 1 is 1.

QUICK QUIZ #13

EASY

5. What is the reciprocal of $\sqrt{\frac{1}{4}}$?

    (A) $\frac{1}{4}$

    (B) $\frac{1}{2}$

    (C) 2

    (D) 4

    (E) 16

MEDIUM

10. $\frac{1}{4}$ is what percent of $\left(\sqrt{5}\right)^3$?

    (A) .25

    (B) $\sqrt{5}$

    (C) 5

    (D) $5\sqrt{50}$

    (E) 50

HARD

13. $\dfrac{\sqrt{6x} \cdot \sqrt{21x} \cdot \sqrt{7x}}{\sqrt{2x}} =$

    (A) $3x$

    (B) $7\sqrt{x}$

    (C) $21x$

    (D) $21\sqrt{x}$

    (E) $7\sqrt{2x}$

Answers and Explanations: Quick Quiz #13

5. **C** $\sqrt{\dfrac{1}{4}} = \dfrac{1}{2}$, and the reciprocal of $\dfrac{1}{2}$ is 2. If you picked (B), you didn't finish the question.

10. **B** $\left(\sqrt{5}\right)^{3} = \sqrt{5 \times 5 \times 5} = 5\sqrt{5}$. Now let's translate the problem as $\dfrac{1}{4} = \dfrac{x}{100} 5\sqrt{5}$. If we solve for x, we get $x = \dfrac{25}{5\sqrt{5}}$ or $5\sqrt{5}$. On the SAT, however, you will never see a square root in the denominator of a fraction. To get the root out of the denominator we multiply $\dfrac{5}{\sqrt{5}} \times \dfrac{\sqrt{5}}{\sqrt{5}} = \dfrac{5\sqrt{5}}{5} = \sqrt{5}$.

13. **C** Remember that you can multiply together everything under the square root signs. This gives us: $\sqrt{\dfrac{6x \times 21x \times 7x}{2x}}$, or we can reduce a $2x$ off top and bottom and get $\sqrt{3 \times 21x \times 7x}$ which is $\sqrt{441x^2}$ or $21\sqrt{x^2}$. Therefore, the whole thing reduces to $21x$.

PROBABILITY AND COMBINATIONS

There won't be many of these problems on the SAT, but you may as well get them right if they show up.

Here's an example:

> If you flip a coin twice, what's the probability of getting 2 heads?

Solution: First write out all the possibilities:

> H – H
>
> H – T
>
> T – T
>
> T – H

That's a total of 4 possibilities, and only 1 is heads-heads. The probability is 1 out of 4, or $\frac{1}{4}$.

Here's another example:

> Mr. Jones must choose 4 of the following 5 flavors of jellybean: apple, berry, coconut, kumquat, and lemon. How many different combinations of flavors can Mr. Jones choose?

4/5

A B C K
A B C L
A B K L
A C K L
B C K L

Solution: Again, write out the possibilities, being careful to go in order so you don't leave anything out. Use the first letter of the flavors as a kind of shorthand:

Flavors:	ABCKL
Possibilities:	ABCK
	ABCL
	ABKL
	ACKL
	BCKL

So there are five possible combinations. Notice that we only went in one direction to get our combinations—the order doesn't matter, and if you go forward and backward (KCAB) you'll get impossibly confused. Being methodical is the key here.

QUICK QUIZ #14

EASY

5. What is the probability of randomly choosing a white marble from a bag that contains 4 white marbles, 2 blue marbles, and 3 green marbles?

(A) $\frac{1}{4}$

(B) $\frac{2}{5}$

(C) $\frac{2}{7}$

(D) $\frac{4}{9}$

(E) $\frac{4}{5}$

MEDIUM

Column A	Column B
steak	french fries
hamburger	spinach
fish	peas
pork chops	salad
	rice

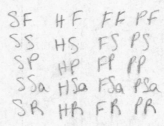

9. If a diner at a certain restaurant may choose 1 item from Column A and 1 item from Column B, how many different combinations may the diner choose?

(A) 5
(B) 9
(C) 15
(D) 20
(E) 25

$C = 1/6$
$L = 2/9$

$\dfrac{1}{6}$ $\dfrac{2}{9}$

$\dfrac{9}{54}$ $\dfrac{12}{54}$

HARD

20. The probability of randomly picking a chocolate cookie out of a certain bag is 1 out of 6, and the probability of picking a lemon cookie is 2 out of 9. If the bag contains only chocolate, vanilla, and lemon cookies, how many vanilla cookies could be in the bag?

(A) 6
(B) 7
(C) 11
(D) 18
(E) 20

$\dfrac{1}{6}$ Choco $\dfrac{2}{9}$ Lem.

	Choc.	Lem.	Van.	Total
ratio	9	12	33	54
multiply				
actual				

$\dfrac{7}{18}$ $\dfrac{11}{18}$

ANSWERS AND EXPLANATIONS: QUICK QUIZ #14

5. **D** The total number of marbles is 9, and 4 of them are white. That means there's a 4-in-9 chance of picking a white marble. Keep in mind that the total goes on the bottom and the part goes on the top, which gives you $\dfrac{4}{9}$. $\dfrac{9}{4}$ isn't one of the choices here, but a lot of people might have wanted to pick it. Be careful.

9. **D** There's a nice shortcut to this kind of combination question: Just add up the total for both columns and multiply. Column A has 4 items and Column B has 5. 5 • 4 = 20. Or you could write out all the combinations, but that would take a while.

20. **C** The probability of picking chocolate is $\dfrac{1}{6}$, and the probability of picking lemon is $\dfrac{2}{9}$. If you add the fractions together, you get $\dfrac{7}{18}$, which is the probability of picking chocolate or lemon. So if there are 18 cookies total, 11 of them would be vanilla.

$\dfrac{1}{6} + \dfrac{2}{9} = \dfrac{7}{18}$ $\dfrac{11}{18}$

SEQUENCES

Most **sequence** problems ask you to find a repeating pattern in a set of numbers.

To attack sequence problems, write out the pattern until it repeats itself. Then extend the pattern out until you can answer the question.

> A rainbow bracelet has a repeating sequence of beads that repeat in the following order: red, orange, yellow, green, blue, violet. What is the color of the 602nd bead?

First write out the pattern:

> Red, orange, yellow, green, blue, violet, red, orange, yellow, green, blue, violet

Notice that the pattern repeats itself after every six beads. That means that every multiple of six will be violet, the sixth bead in the pattern. What multiple of six is closest to 602? 600 is a good choice. Thus…

600	601	602
Violet	Red	Orange

The 602nd bead is orange.

QUICK QUIZ #15

EASY

4. A certain list contains 11 consecutive multiples of 3. The first number is 21. What is the middle number?

   (A) 26
   (B) 27
   (C) 36
   (D) 39
   (E) 51

MEDIUM

11. The first three numbers of a sequence are 1, 3, and 5, respectively. Every number in the sequence beyond the first three numbers can be found by taking the three preceding numbers, subtracting the second from the first, and adding the third. Which of the following is the sum of the first 40 numbers of the above sequence?

    (A)   6
    (B) 12
    (C) 24
    (D) 120
    (E) 480

ANSWERS AND EXPLANATIONS: QUICK QUIZ #15

4. **C** The middle number in the list is the sixth term. Don't write out all the terms; just list them up to the sixth one: 21, 24, 27, 30, 33, **36.**

11. **D** If you follow the sequence out, the next number is 3, and then if you keep following the instructions, the sequence repeats itself (1,3,5,3 1,3,5,3 1,3,5,3 1,3,5,3) in sets of 4. So, take the first four numbers and find the sum (12) and multiply by 10 since we actually want the first 40 numbers.

Algebra

In the section on strategy, we gave you some ways to avoid algebra altogether—but you still need to be able to work with simple equations and review some other algebraic principles that don't exactly crop up in everyday life.

SIMPLE EQUATIONS

Sometimes you can plug in with these, sometimes not. You will definitely need to be comfortable manipulating equations to do well on the SAT.

To solve a simple equation, get the variable on one side of the equals sign and the numbers on the other.

$$8x - 4 = 12 + x$$
$$8x - 4 = 12$$
$$8x = 16$$
$$x = 2$$

We just added 4 to both sides and subtracted x from both sides. Then we divided both sides by 8. You can add, subtract, multiply, or divide either side of an equation, but remember that what you do to one side you have to do to the other.

Polynomial equations look tricky but follow all the same rules of simple equations. You can add and subtract like terms—terms that have the same variables raised to the same powers.

What is the value of z if $3z + 4z + 7z = -42$?

In this case, the terms all have the same variable and are all to the same power. Thus, we can combine them to get $14z = -42$.

Now we'll divide each side by 14 and get $z = -14$.

To solve a proportion, cross-multiply:

$$\frac{3}{x} = \frac{1}{2}$$

$$x = 6$$

Remember that you can't cancel across an equals sign!

QUICK QUIZ #1

EASY

3. If $\dfrac{3x}{5} = \dfrac{x+2}{3}$, what is the value of x?

   (A) $\dfrac{1}{2}$

   (B) 1

   (C) 2

   (D) $2\dfrac{1}{2}$

   (E) 3

Handwritten: $9x = 5x + 10$ $4x = 10$ $x = 10/4$

MEDIUM

6. If $\dfrac{5}{x} = \dfrac{y}{10}$ and $x - y = y$, then $y + x =$

   (A) 5
   (B) 10
   (C) 15
   (D) 25
   (E) 50

Handwritten: $xy = 50$ $x = 50/y$ $y = 50/x$

$\dfrac{50}{y} - y = y$ $y = 5$ $x = 50/5 = 10$ 15

$\dfrac{50}{y} = 2y$ $50 = 2y^2$ $25 = y^2$

HARD

14. If $\dfrac{a+1}{b+1} = \dfrac{a}{b}$, then $(a+b)(a-b) =$

   (A) −1
   (B) 0
   (C) 1
   (D) 2
   (E) It cannot be determined from the information given.

Handwritten: $ba + a = ba + b$ $a = b$ $(a+b)(a-b)$ $a^2 + ba - ba + b^2$ $a^2 - b^2 = 0$

3. **D** Cross-multiply, and you get $9x = 5(x + 2)$

$$9x = 5x + 10$$

$$4x = 10$$

$$x = 2\frac{1}{2}$$

6. **C** Plug in 10 for x and 5 for y. Both equations are satisfied by those numbers. So $y + x = 15$.

Just to show you the kind of algebra that you'd be forced to do if you didn't plug in—first, cross-multiply to get $xy = 50$. Your other equation is $x - y = y$, so $x = 2y$. Substitute that x into the first equation, and you get $2y^2 = 50$, or $y^2 = 25$. So $y = 5$. Substitute $y = 5$ into either equation and solve for x. You get $x = 10$. Now add 'em up and you get $x + y = 15$. Lots more work, huh? If you don't plug in when you can, it's really going to slow you down. And that's the least of it. You're also more likely to get the question wrong because the algebra takes so many steps.

14. **B** Sometimes you can't plug in because it's too hard to find numbers that satisfy the equation. So this time we have to do the algebra. First, cross-multiply: $ab + a = ab + b$, so $a = b$. The question asks for

$(a + b)(a - b)$. Now plug in. If $a = 2$ and $b = 2$, then $(a - b)$ is 0 and the whole thing is 0.

Oh, did you pick (E)? Never pick "It cannot be determined" if you're dazed and confused. Not on a hard question. That answer is correct when you can get more than one right answer, and that usually only happens on medium questions.

QUADRATIC EQUATIONS

Even the name is scary. What does it mean, anyway? No matter. All you need to know are a few simple things: factoring and recognizing perfect squares.

To factor, first draw a pair of empty parentheses. Deal with the first term, then the signs, then the last term. For example:

$$x^2 + x - 12 \qquad (\quad)(\quad)$$
$$(x\quad)(x\quad) \ldots \text{first term}$$
$$(x +\quad)(x -\quad) \ldots \text{signs}$$
$$(x + 4)(x - 3) \ldots \text{last term}$$

Check your factoring by multiplying the terms:

first term = $x \times x = x^2$
inner term = $4x$
outer term = $-3x$
last term = $4 \times -3 = -12$

Then add them up:

$$x^2 + 4x + -3x + -12 = x^2 + x - 12$$

Some guidelines:
If the last term is positive, your signs will be either +, + or −, −.
If the last term is negative, your signs will be +, −.
Your first try may not be right—don't be afraid to mess around with it a little.

To recognize the difference of two squares, memorize the following:

$$(x + y)(x - y) = x^2 - y^2$$

This format works whether you have variables, as above, or numbers:

$$57^2 - 43^2 = (57 + 43)(57 - 43) = 100 \times 14 = 1400$$

One more thing—memorize the following:

$$(x + y)^2 = (x + y)(x + y) = x^2 + 2xy + y^2$$

$$(x - y)^2 = (x - y)(x - y) = x^2 - 2xy + y^2$$

TIP:
When you see anything that looks like one form of these expressions, try converting to its other form. That should lead you straight to the correct answer.

QUICK QUIZ #2

EASY

[handwritten: $\frac{(x+2)(x+3)}{x^2+2x+3x+6}$]

7. If $\dfrac{x^2+5x+6}{x+2} = 12$, then $x =$

[handwritten: $x+3=12$, $x=9$]

(A) –2
(B) 2
(C) 3
(D) 6
(E) 9 *(circled)*

MEDIUM

[handwritten: $a = 3+b$ $-b = 3-a$ $b = -3+a$ $b = a-3$]

15. If $a - b = 3$ and $a^2 - b^2 = 21$, then $a =$

(A) –3
(B) –2
(C) 2
(D) 5 *(circled)*
(E) 7

*[handwritten:
$(a+b)(a-b) = 21$
$(a+b)(3) = 21$
$3a+3b = 21$
$3a+3(a-3) = 21$
$3a+3a-9 = 21$
$6a-9 = 21$]*

HARD

20. If $x < 0$ and $(2x - 1)^2 = 25$, then $x^2 =$

(A) –4
(B) –2 *(circled)*
(C) 3
(D) 4 *(circled)*
(E) 9

*[handwritten:
$x = -$
$(2x-1)(2x-1)$
$4x^2-2x-2x+1$
$4x^2-4x+1 = 25$
$4x^2-4x-24 =$
$x = -2$]*

Answers and Explanations: Quick Quiz #2

7. **E** First, factor the expression to $(x + 3)(x + 2)$. Now you have

$\dfrac{(x+3)(x+2)}{x+2} = 12$. The $(x + 2)$ cancels, and you have $x + 3 = 12$, so

$x = 9$. Or you could plug in: If $x = 9$, $\dfrac{9^2 + 5(9) + 6}{9 + 2} = 12$, or $\dfrac{132}{11} = 12$.

It looks funny, but it works.

15. **D** Factor $a^2 - b^2$ to equal $(a + b)(a - b) = 21$. If $a - b = 3$, then $a + b = 7$. Here you could do one of two things. You can try some different numbers and see what satisfies both simple equations, or you could add the two equations together and get $2a = 10$, $a = 5$.

20. **D** Lots of algebra:

$$(2x-1)^2 = 25$$
$$(2x-1)(2x-1) = 25$$
$$4x^2 - 4x + 1 = 25$$
$$4x^2 - 4x - 24 = 0$$
$$x^2 - x - 6 = 0$$
$$(x - 3)(x + 2) = 0$$

So x can be 3 or –2. If x is negative, it has to be –2, and $-2^2 = 4$. You could also Plug in, but you have to remember that the question asks for x^2, not x. That means (D) and (E) are good answers to try, since they're squares.

Don't forget that one of your main jobs on the SAT is following directions. If you picked (B) or (C), we suspect you did most of the problem correctly but forgot that x is negative, or failed to square x. Don't let carelessness rob you of your hard-earned points!

SIMULTANEOUS EQUATIONS

Two different equations, two different variables. You will not usually have to solve for both variables.

To solve simultaneous equations, stack 'em up, and either add or subtract:

If $2x + 3y = 12$ and $3x - 3y = -2$, what is the value of x?

$$
\begin{array}{r}
2x + 3y = 12 \\
+\ 3x - 3y = -2 \\
\hline
5x = 10 \\
x = 2
\end{array}
$$

If we had subtracted, we'd have gotten $-x + 6y = 14$, which wouldn't get us anywhere. If you choose the wrong operation, no big deal, just try the other one.

> **TIP:**
> Don't automatically start solving for x and y—you may not need to. Focus on what the question is specifically asking.

QUICK QUIZ #3

MEDIUM

9. If $3x + 3y = 4$ and $2x - 3y = 1$, what is the value of x?

   (A) $\dfrac{1}{3}$

   (B) 1

   (C) 3

   (D) 5

   (E) 6

10. At a restaurant, 2 orders of pancakes and 1 order of bacon costs $4.92. If 2 orders of bacon cost $3.96, what does 1 order of pancakes cost?

(A) $.96
(B) $1.47
(C) $1.98
(D) $2.94
(E) $3.20

11. If $3x + 5y = 15$ and $x - 2y = 10$, then $2x + 7y =$

(A) 5
(B) 10
(C) 15
(D) 25
(E) 50

ANSWERS AND EXPLANATIONS: QUICK QUIZ #3

9. **B** Stack 'em and add:

$$3x + 3y = 4$$
$$+\ 2x - 3y = 1$$
$$\overline{5x = 5}$$
$$x = 1$$

10. **B** If 2 orders of bacon cost $3.96, divide by 2 to get the cost of 1 order of bacon. That's $1.98. If 2 orders of pancakes and 1 order of bacon costs $4.92, we can subtract the $1.98 and get $2.94, which is the cost of 2 orders of pancakes. Divide by 2 to get 1 order of pancakes. That's $1.47.

The simultaneous equations would be $2p + b = 4.92$ and $2b = 3.96$. Solve for b and then use that number to solve for p in the first equation. It's even possible to plug in on this question, but the numbers are so irregular and hard to work with, it probably isn't worth it.

$$3x + 5y = 15 \qquad 3x + 5y = 15$$

11. **A** Stack 'em and subtract: $-(x - 2y = 10) \qquad \dfrac{-\ x - 2y = -10}{2x + 7y = 5}$

That's it. You don't have to solve for x or y individually. Less work is good. (Be careful with the signs when you subtract one equation from another.)

[handwritten: if you multiply or divide by a negative # the sign changes direction]

INEQUALITIES

Treat these just like equations, but remember one rule: **If you multiply or divide by a negative number, the sign changes direction.**

$$x + 6 > 10 \qquad\qquad 2x > 16 \qquad\qquad -2x > 16$$
$$x > 4 \qquad\qquad\quad x > 8 \qquad\qquad\quad x < -8$$

> **BEWARE:**
> It's very easy to mix up the direction of the > or < sign. Be extra careful.

QUICK QUIZ #4

[handwritten: $3x + 7 < 5x - 4$]
[handwritten: $11 < 2x$]
[handwritten: $11/2 < x$]

EASY

3. If $3x + 7 < 5x - 4$, then

   [handwritten: A]

   (A) $\dfrac{11}{2} < x$

   (B) $x < \dfrac{3}{2}$

   (C) $x < \dfrac{11}{8}$

   (D) $x > \dfrac{2}{3}$

   (E) $\dfrac{11}{2} > x$

   [handwritten:
   $3x + 7 < 5x - 4$
   $3x + 11 < 5x$
   $11 < 2x$
   $\dfrac{11}{2} < x$ *]*

MEDIUM

11. If $3b + 8 > 6 + 2b$, and b is a negative integer,
    then $b =$

    (A) 1
    (B) 0
    (C) −1
    (D) −2
    (E) −3

    [handwritten:
    $3b + 8 > 6 + 2b$
    $3b + 2 > 2b$
    $2 > -b$
    $-2 < b$ *]*

    [handwritten:
    $3b + 8 > 6 + 2b$
    $b > -2$
    $b = -$ *]*

$0 < s < 4$

$s = 2$

$3t - 3 > 6s + 9$
$t - 5s < 12$

$3t - 6s > 12$
$t - 5s < 12$

$3t - 12 > 12$
$t - 10 < 12$
$18 - 12 > 12$
$6 - 10 < 12$

HARD

$s = 2$

20. If $3t - 3 > 6s + 9$ and $t - 5s < 12$, and s is a positive integer less than 4, then t could be any of the following EXCEPT

$3t - 3 > 6s - 9$
$t - 5s < 12$

A

(A) 6
(B) 8
(C) 10
(D) 12
(E) 23

$t - 10 < 12$
$t < 22$

$2 < t < 22$

$3t - 3 = 12 - 9$
$3t - 3 = 3$
$\dfrac{3t = 6}{3} \quad \dfrac{}{3}$
$t > 2$

ANSWERS AND EXPLANATIONS: QUICK QUIZ #4

3. **A** Treat the inequality just like an equation—subtract $3x$ from both sides, and you get $7 < 2x - 4$. Add 4 to both sides, and you get $11 < 2x$. Divide through by 2, which leaves you with $\dfrac{11}{2} < x$.

11. **C** Move the bs to one side and the integers to the other, and you get $b > -2$. If b is a negative integer, the only possibility is -1.

20. **A** Manipulate the inequalities so that they're more manageable. The first one can be reduced to $t - 1 > 2s + 3$, or $t > 2s + 4$. The second inequality can be manipulated to $t < 12 + 5s$. Now let's plug in. If s is a positive integer less than 4, start with the first possible value for s, which is $s = 1$. Plugged into both inequalities, that gives you $t > 6$ and $t < 17$. Cross out (B), (C), and (D). Now try the highest possible value for s, which is $s = 3$. That gives you $t > 10$ and $t < 27$. Cross out (E), and pick the answer that's left: (A).

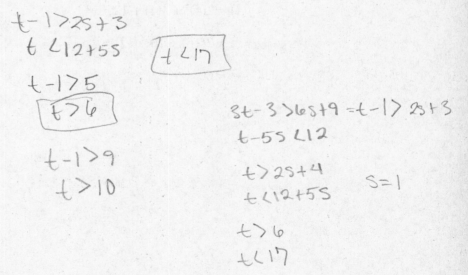

$t - 1 > 2s + 3$
$t < 12 + 5s$ $\boxed{t < 17}$

$t - 1 > 5$
$\boxed{t > 6}$

$t - 1 > 9$
$t > 10$

$3t - 3 > 6s + 9 = t - 1 > 2s + 3$
$t - 5s < 12$

$t > 2s + 4$
$t < 12 + 5s$ $s = 1$

$t > 6$
$t < 17$

FUNCTIONS

Functions come in many forms on the SAT, but all of them require you to follow directions.

ETS may make up a math term you've never heard before. Relax, you didn't miss anything exciting in algebra class. Just follow the directions given by the definition of the term.

> The "prime component" of an integer is defined as the sum of all the prime factors of that integer. What is the prime component of 39?

First, break down 39 into its prime factors, 3 and 13. Next, find the sum: $3 + 13 = 16$. That's all there is to it.

Alternately, ETS may designate a function by using a strange-looking symbol. For example:

> For any integer t, $[t] = t^2 + t$. What is the value of $[4] - [3]$?

Solution: Let's take $[4]$ first. The direction tells us to square the number, and then add the number, so $4^2 + 4 = 20$. Now let's do the same for $[3]$. $3^2 + 3 = 12$. So $[4] - [3] = 20 - 12 = 8$.

Finally, ETS may resort to using actual mathematical functions, indicated by the expression $f(x)$.

> If $f(x) = 2x^2 + 4x + 12$, what is the value of $f(4)$?

Don't be distracted by the fancy symbols; just pop the number into the function and crank out the answer. We want the $f(4)$, so wherever there is an x in the function, we'll replace it with a 4.

$$f(4) = 2(4)^2 + 4(4) + 12$$

$$= 2(16) + 16 + 12$$

$$= 60$$

$$[t] = t^2 + t$$
$$[4] = 16 + 4 = 20$$
$$[3] = 9 + 3 = 12 \qquad = 8$$

QUICK QUIZ # 5

EASY

(handwritten, top right)
$f(x) = 2x^2 + 3$
$21 = 2x^2 + 3$
$0 = 2x^2 - 18$

4. If $f(x) = 2x^2 + 3$, for which of the following values of x does $f(x) = 21$?

    (A) −9
    (B) −3
    (C)   0
    (D)   1
    (E)   9

(handwritten) B

(handwritten)
$2x^2 + 3 = 21$
$2x^2 = 18$
$x^2 = 9$

MEDIUM

16. If $[a + b] = a^2 - b^2$, then $\dfrac{[x+y]}{x+y} =$

    (A) $x + y$
    (B) $x - y$
    (C) $2x - 2y$
    (D) 1
    (E) $(x + y)^2$

(handwritten) B

(handwritten)
$\dfrac{x^2 - y^2}{x+y} \qquad \dfrac{(x+y)(x-y)}{x+y} \qquad x - y$

$[a + b] = a^2 - b^2$

$[x + y] = \dfrac{x^2 + y^2}{x + y} \qquad \dfrac{(x+y)(x-y)}{x+y}$

HARD

19. The height of the steam burst of a certain geyser varies with the length of time since the previous steam burst. The longer the time since the last burst, the greater the height of the steam burst. If t is the time in hours since the previous steam burst and H is the height in meters of the steam burst, which of the following could express the relationship of t and H?

    (A) $H(t) = \dfrac{1}{2}(t - 7)$

    (B) $H(t) = \dfrac{2}{t-7}$

    (C) $H(t) = 2 - (t - 7)$

    (D) $H(t) = 7 - 2t$

    (E) $H(t) = \dfrac{2}{7t}$

(handwritten) A

(handwritten) H↑ T↑   H(t)

Answers and Explanations: Quick Quiz #5

4. **B** In this case, plug in answer choices for the value of x, starting with answer (C). Plugging in 0 for x gives you $f(0) = 2(0)^2 + 3 = 3$. But you want $f(x) = 21$, so eliminate (C). Now try (B): $f(-3) = 21$, so this is the right answer. Alternatively, set $f(x) = 21$, and solve $21 = 2x^2 + 3$.

16. **B** $[x + y] = x^2 - y^2$, which factors to $(x + y)(x - y)$. When you divide, the $(x + y)$ term cancels, and you're left with $x - y$.

19. **A** The relationship is the greater the time, the greater the height. So, the correct function is one that yields a greater H as you increase t.

    Try plugging in for t in the functions to see which one increases as t increases. So, try $t = 10$ and $t = 20$. Only (A) has a greater H for $t = 10$ than it does for $t = 20$. That is $\frac{1}{2}(10 - 7) > \frac{1}{2}(20 - 7)$. So, (A) is correct.

4
Geometry

You're not going to believe how simple this is—no proofs, no trig, no parabolas. Just a few rules, a couple of formulas, and your common sense. And don't forget about estimating.

DEFINITIONS

arc	part of a circumference
area	the space inside a two-dimensional figure
bisect	cut in two equal parts
chord	a line that goes through a circle, but does not go through the center; it will always be shorter than the diameter
circumference	the distance around a circle
diagonal	a line from one corner of a square to its opposite corner
diameter	a line directly through the center of a circle; the longest line you can draw in a circle
equidistant	exactly in the middle
equilateral	a triangle with three equal sides, therefore three equal angles (60 degrees each)
hypotenuse	the longest leg of a right triangle, opposite the right angle
isosceles	a triangle with two equal sides and two equal angles
parallel	lines that will never intersect (think railroad tracks)
perimeter	the distance around a figure
perpendicular	two lines that intersect to form 90-degree angles
quadrilateral	any four-sided figure
radius	a line from the center of a circle to the edge of the circle (half the diameter)
volume	the space inside a three-dimensional figure

LINES AND ANGLES

A line has 180°, so the angles formed by any cut to your line will add up to 180°:

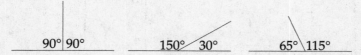

Two intersecting lines form a pair of **vertical angles**, that are equal:

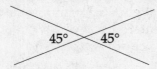

Parallel lines cut by a third line will form two kinds of angles: big ones and little ones. All the big ones are equal to each other; all the little ones are equal to each other. Any big angle plus any little angle will equal 180°:

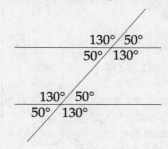

QUICK QUIZ #1

EASY

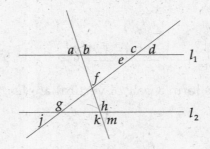

4. In the figure above, l_1 is parallel to l_2. Which of the following angles are NOT equal?

(A) *c* and *g*
(B) *b* and *h*
(C) *a* and *m*
(D) *a* and *k*
(E) *d* and *j*

MEDIUM

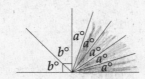

10. In the figure above, what is the value of $4a - b$?

(A) 18°
(B) 27°
(C) 45°
(D) 54°
(E) 115°

b = 45
a = 18
72 − 45 = 27

HARD

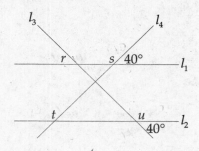

Note: Figure not drawn to scale.

18. Which of the following must be true?

(A) $l_1 \parallel l_2$
(B) l_3 bisects l_4
(C) $r = 40°$
(D) $s = t$
(E) $u = 140°$

ANSWERS AND EXPLANATIONS: QUICK QUIZ #1

4. **D** Start with (A) and cross off as you go along. In (D), $a = m$, not k. Keep in mind that the two lines cutting through l_1 and l_2 aren't parallel, and so the angles made by one line have no relationship to the angles made by the other line.

10. **B** Estimate first. Outline the measurement of four of the a's. That's about 60. Now pretend you are subtracting b, about 45. How much is left? Not so much, right? Cross out (D) and (E). Now do the math: $2b = 90°$, so $b = 45°$. $5a = 90$, so $a = 18°$. Now plug those numbers into the equation: $4(18) - 45 = 27$.

18. **E** This question is actually very easy, as long as you don't pick the first answer that looks halfway decent and not even get to (E). Angle u has to be 140° because it's on a straight line with the angle marked 40°. All the other answers look like they're true, but we can't know for certain. The only thing you know for sure is that angles on the same line add up to 180°, and vertical angles are equal. None of these lines are necessarily parallel, so you can't assume anything else.

TRIANGLES

Triangles have 180°.

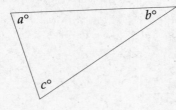

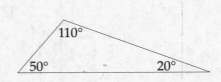

$$a + b + c = 180°$$ $$50° + 20° + 110° = 180°$$

Area = $\dfrac{1}{2}bh.$

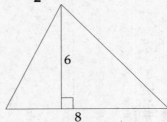

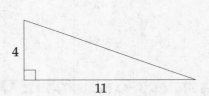

area = $\dfrac{1}{2}(8)(6) = 24$ area = $\dfrac{1}{2}(11)(4) = 22$

Perimeter: Add up the sides.

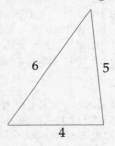

Perimeter = 15

Right triangles have a right, or 90°, angle:

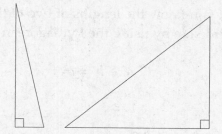

Isosceles triangles have two equal sides and two equal angles:

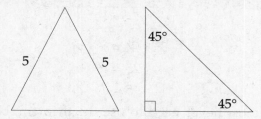

Equilateral triangles have three equal sides and three equal angles:

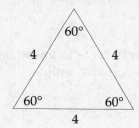

Similar triangles have equal angles and proportional sides:

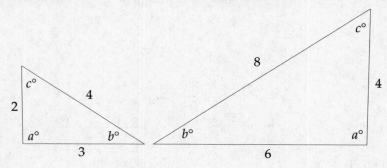

THE WONDERFUL WORLD OF RIGHT TRIANGLES

For any right triangle, if you know the lengths of two of the sides, you can figure out the length of the third side by using the Pythagorean theorem:

$$a^2 + b^2 = c^2$$

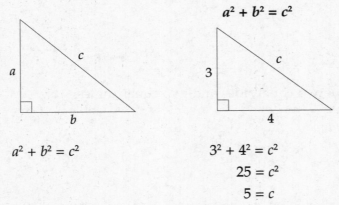

$$a^2 + b^2 = c^2$$

$$3^2 + 4^2 = c^2$$
$$25 = c^2$$
$$5 = c$$

However, you almost never need to use the theorem, because almost every right angle you will find will have lengths that fit one of these common Pythagorean triples.

3:4:5   6:8:10   5:12:13

In two special cases, you only have to know one side to figure out the other two, because the sides are in a constant ratio.

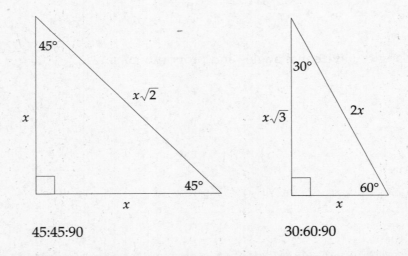

45:45:90   30:60:90

TIP:
Memorize the shapes of these two triangles, and it will be easier to recognize them on the SAT. A 45:45:90 triangle is half of a square, and a 30:60:90 triangle is half of an equilateral triangle.

QUICK QUIZ #2

EASY

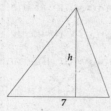

$\frac{1}{2}7h=21$

$n=21\left(\frac{2}{7}\right)$

5. If the triangle above has an area of 21, then *h* equals

(A) 3
(B) 4
(C) 6
(D) 7
(E) 8

MEDIUM

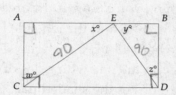

90

90

14. If *ABCD* is a rectangle, what is the value of $w + x + y + z$?

(A) 90
(B) 150
(C) 180
(D) 190
(E) 210

HARD

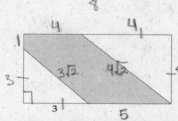

Note: Figure not drawn to scale.

$4+1+3\sqrt{2}+5+4\sqrt{2}$

$10+7\sqrt{2}$

$A=32$

$P=?$

20. If the rectangle above has an area of 32, and the unshaded triangles are isosceles, what is the perimeter of the shaded area?

(A) 16
(B) $10 + 7\sqrt{2}$
(C) $10 + 12\sqrt{2}$
(D) 32
(E) $70\sqrt{2}$

5. **C** Estimate first—it's drawn to scale. If the base is 7, how long does the height look? About the same? Cross out at least (A) and (E), and (B) if you're feeling confident. Now do the math: area = $\frac{1}{2}$ bh, so $\frac{1}{2}$ $(7h) = 21$, and $h = 6$. It would be easy to pick (A) if you weren't paying attention, because $7 \times 3 = 21$, and so it seems appealing. But only if you aren't paying attention. And we know you are.

14. **C** If you picked (A) or (E), you didn't estimate. Very bad. See how the rectangle is cut up into three triangles? Each of those triangles has 180°. Both of the triangles with marked angles also have right angles because they're corners of a rectangle. So $\triangle ACE + \triangle EBD = 360°$. Subtract the two right angles, and you're left with 180°.

20. **B** First write in everything you know: If the area is 32, the length is 8. That means the base is $3 + 5$ and the left side is $1 + 3$. The triangles in opposing corners are both 45:45:90 triangles: The one on the base has a hypotenuse of $3\sqrt{2}$, and the one with sides of 4 has a hypotenuse of $4\sqrt{2}$. Add up all the sides of the shaded part, and you get $10 + 7\sqrt{2}$.

Here's how it should look:

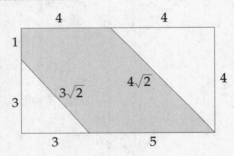

TRIGONOMETRY

Trigonometry problems on the SAT test your knowledge of sines, cosines, and tangents.

Here's how you find them:

$$\text{sine} = \frac{opposite}{hypotenuse} \qquad \text{cosine} = \frac{adjacent}{hypotenuse} \qquad \text{tangent} = \frac{opposite}{adjacent}$$

Use the following mnemonic to help you recall these relationships.

SOHCAHTOA

Use trigonometry only as a last resort. Many triangle problems can be solved by using the Pythagorean theorem or the special right triangles.

QUICK QUIZ #3

MEDIUM

11. Mathias looks up at a certain time of day and sees that the sun is at an angle of 32° with the horizontal. If Mathias is approximately 6 feet tall, how long is his shadow?

(A)   3.2 feet
(B)   3.7 feet
(C)   5.1 feet
(D)   9.6 feet
(E)   12.0 feet

(handwritten: $\tan 32 x = 6$; $x = 6/\tan 32$; $\tan(32) = \dfrac{6}{x}$)

HARD

16. Attalah is trying to figure out how the height of her building and the building next door compare. She knows that if she stands at the edge of the roof of her building closest to the building next door and looks up at the roof of the building next door, she must look up at an angle of 13° with the horizontal. If she stands at the base of her building closest to the building next door and looks up at the roof of the building next door, she must look up at an angle of 72°. If Attalah knows that the building next door is 800 feet tall, approximately how much shorter, in feet, is her building than the building next door?

(A) 45.5 feet
(B) 60.0 feet
(C) 200.7 feet
(D) 253.3 feet
(E) 260.2 feet

20. Petra watches a plane flying overhead at a constant altitude of 26,400 feet. When she first looks up at the plane, she sees it at an angle of 50° above the horizontal. If 5 minutes later she looks up and sees the plane at and angle of 7.85°, approximately how fast is plane traveling in miles per hour? (Note: 5,280 feet = 1 mile)

(A) 50.3 mph
(B) 192.5 mph
(C) 384.7 mph
(D) 435.2 mph
(E) 487.5 mph

(handwritten work:)

$26,400$

$50°$

22152.23

$\tan 50 = \dfrac{26,400}{x}$

$(\tan 50)x = 26400$

$26,400$

$7.85°$

$191,481.806$

$\tan 7.85 = \dfrac{26400}{x}$

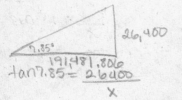

$\dfrac{169329.576 \text{ ft}}{5 \text{ min}} \left| \dfrac{1 \text{ mi}}{5,280 \text{ ft}} \right| \dfrac{60 \text{ min}}{1 \text{ hr}} = 384.83$

Answers and Explanations: Quick Quiz #3

11. **D** In order to solve for the length of the shadow, set up a triangle with sides of 6 feet and the length of the shadow. The angle above the horizontal would be 32°. In order to solve, use $\tan(32°) = \dfrac{6\,\text{ft}}{x}$. x ends up as 9.6 feet.

16. **B** In order to find the difference in heights between the buildings, it's important to first find out how far apart the two buildings are. If Attalah must look up at the building next door at 72° when she is standing on the ground, and the building next door is 800 feet tall, you can find out how far apart the buildings are by using tangents. Set it up like this: $\tan(72°) = \dfrac{800\,\text{ft}}{x}$, where x is the distance between the buildings. x is approximately 260 feet. Now that you know how far apart the buildings are, you can use the angle that Attalah views the building at from the roof of her own building to see how much taller the other building is. Since the buildings are 260 feet apart, and the she must look up at an angle of 13° to see the roof of the building next door, use tangent again like this: $\tan(13°) = \dfrac{y}{260\,\text{ft}}$, where y is the difference in height of the two buildings.

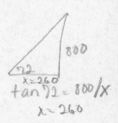

$\tan 72 = 800/x$
$x = 260$

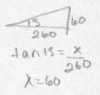

$\tan 13 = \dfrac{x}{260}$
$x = 60$

20. **C** The best way to approach this problem is to draw a picture, as shown below.

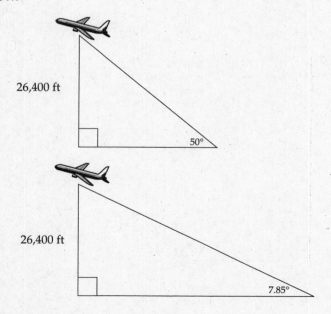

26,400 ft   50°

26,400 ft   7.85°

Start by finding the complementary angle to 50°, so that you can deal with the smaller of the two triangles. Draw in 40°, and since you know the height, find the other leg of the triangle. Convert the height to miles before you begin: 24,600 feet = x miles × 5280 feet, so x = 5 miles. So $\tan(40°) = \dfrac{d}{5}$, and d = 4.2 miles. Now find the other leg of the larger triangle, by following the same process. The complementary angle to 7.85° is 82.15°. So $\tan(82.15°) = \dfrac{d}{5}$, so d = 36.26 miles. Therefore the total distance that the plane travels in 5 minutes is about 32.06 miles. Now just convert this to miles per hour. If the plane can cover 32.06 miles in 5 minutes, how far can it go in 60 minutes? Set up a ratio and solve: $\dfrac{32.06 \text{ miles}}{5 \min} = \dfrac{y \text{ miles}}{60 \min}$. y = 384.72, or close to 384.7 miles per hour. This would also be a good problem to consider skipping.

CIRCLES

Circles have 360°. Area = πr^2.

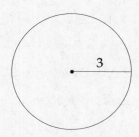

Circumference = $2\pi r$

$r = 3$

$C = 2\pi(3) = 6\pi$

$A = \pi(3)^2 = 9\pi$

TIP:

For any pie slice of a circle, the central angle, arc, and area are in proportion to the whole circle.

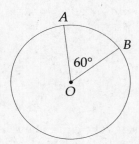

$\dfrac{60°}{360°} = \dfrac{1}{6}$, so arc AB is $\dfrac{1}{6}$ of the circumference, and pie slice AOB is $\dfrac{1}{6}$ of the total area.

QUICK QUIZ #4

EASY

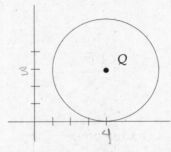

4. Center Q of the circle above has coordinates of (4, 3). What is the circumference of the circle?

   (A) π
   (B) 2π
   (C) 6π
   (D) 8π
   (E) 9π

   $2\pi r$
   $2\pi 3 = 6\pi$

MEDIUM

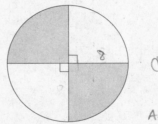

13. If the circumference of the circle above is 16π, what is the total area of the shaded regions?

   (A) 64π
   (B) 32π
   (C) 12π
   (D) 8π
   (E) 4π

   $C = 2\pi r = 16\pi$
   $2\pi r = 2\pi 8$
   $r = 8$
   $A = \pi r^2 = 64\pi$

   $\dfrac{64\pi}{4} = 16\pi$

HARD

20. One circle has a radius of r, and another circle has a radius of $2r$. The area of the larger circle is how many times the area of the smaller circle?

   $r = 2$

   (A) .5
   (B) 1.5
   (C) 2
   (D) 3
   (E) 4

   $A = \pi 4$

   $A = \pi 16$

Answers and Explanations: Quick Quiz #4

4. **C** The easiest way to solve this is simply to count the number of units in the radius, which is 3. Make sure you draw a radius on the diagram—if you draw it perpendicular to the y-axis you'll be able to count the units with no problem. If you picked (E), you found the area. Read the question carefully and give 'em what they ask for.

13. **B** The circumference is 16π, so use the circumference formula to get the radius: $2\pi r = 16\pi$, and $r = 8$. The area of the whole circle is $\pi r^2 = \pi(8)^2 = 64\pi$. Hold on—don't pick (A). At this point, you could happily estimate the shaded area as half the circle and pick (B). (Nothing else is close.) In fact, the shaded area is exactly half of the circle because each marked angle is 90°, which makes each of those pie slices $\dfrac{90°}{360°}$ or $\dfrac{1}{4}$ of the circle. So two of them make up $\dfrac{1}{2}$ of the circle, or 32π. Trust what your eyes tell you.

20. **E** Plug in. If $r = 2$, then the area of the small circle is 4π. The radius of the second circle is 2(2) or 4, so the area is 16π. The larger circle is 4 times as big as the smaller circle. (Don't you just love to plug in?)

> **TIP:**
> Notice how the hard question doesn't give you a picture or any real numbers to use. So draw the picture and make up your own numbers. Try to visualize the problem. Plugging In works just as well on geometry problems as it does on algebra problems.

Note: A very common careless error on circle problems is getting the area and circumference mixed up. Don't worry! The formulas are printed on the first page of each math section in case you forgot them. (It's better, of course, if you can memorize the formulas.)

QUADRILATERALS

Quadrilaterals have 360°.

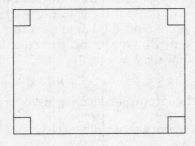 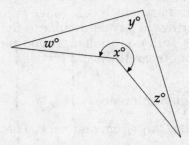

$$90° + 90° + 90° + 90° = 360°$$ $$w + x + y + z = 360°$$

Perimeter: Add up the sides.

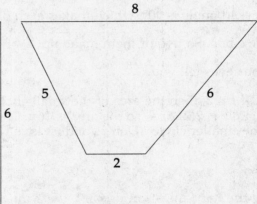

$P = 16$ $P = 21$

PARALLELOGRAMS

Parallelograms have two pairs of parallel lines, but no right angles.

Area = Base × Height

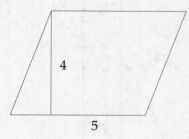

$A = bh$ $\qquad\qquad$ $A = (5)(4)$ $\qquad\qquad$ $A = 20$

Rectangles have four 90° angles and two pairs of parallel lines.

Area = $l \times w$

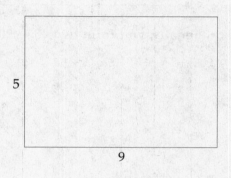

$A = lw$

$A = (9)(5)$

$A = 45$

TIP:
Note that there's no relationship between the perimeter of a rectangle and its area.

$P = 36$ $\qquad\qquad\qquad$ $P = 36$

$A = 17$ $\qquad\qquad\qquad$ $A = 81$

Squares have four 90° angles and two pairs of parallel lines, all the same length.

Area = $l \times w$ or s^2

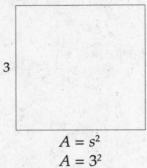

$A = s^2$
$A = 3^2$
$A = 9$

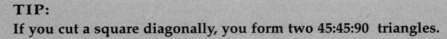

TIP:
If you cut a square diagonally, you form two 45:45:90 triangles.

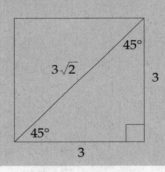

QUICK QUIZ #5

EASY

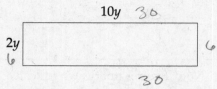

10y   30

2y
6

30

6

30

3. If $y = 3$, what is the perimeter of the figure above?

(A) 12
(B) 20
(C) 50
(D) 60
(E) 72

MEDIUM

9. What is the area of a square with a diagonal 5?

(A) 10

(B) 12.5

(C) 25

(D) $25\sqrt{2}$

(E) $50\sqrt{2}$

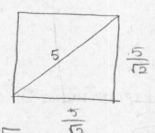

5

$\frac{5}{\sqrt{2}}$

$\frac{5}{\sqrt{2}}$

$5 = x\sqrt{2}$

$\frac{5}{\sqrt{2}} = x$

$\frac{5}{\sqrt{2}} \cdot \frac{5}{\sqrt{2}} = \frac{25}{2} = 12.5$

HARD

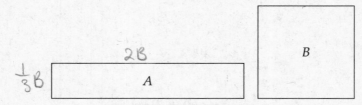

Note: Figures not drawn to scale.

12. The length of Rectangle A is $\frac{1}{3}$ the length of Rectangle B, and the width of A is twice the width of B. What is the ratio of the area of A to the area of B?

(A) $\frac{1}{3}$

(B) $\frac{2}{3}$

(C) 1

(D) $\frac{3}{2}$

(E) $\frac{3}{4}$

[handwritten:]
$A = L \cdot W$
$A = 2 \cdot \frac{1}{3} = \frac{2}{8} B$
B length = 6   B width = 4
A length = 2   A width = 8
$2 \cdot 8 = 16$ $6 \cdot 4 = 24$ $\frac{16}{24} = \frac{2}{3}$

ANSWERS AND EXPLANATIONS: QUICK QUIZ #25

3. **E** Figure out the dimensions of the rectangle if $y = 3$. That makes the length $10 \times 3 = 30$, and the width $2 \times 3 = 6$. Write those numbers on the diagram where they belong. To get the perimeter, add up all the sides. $30 + 30 + 6 + 6 = 72$.

9. **B** If the square has diagonal 5, then 5 is also the hypotenuse of the two 45:45:90 right triangles that are formed by the diagonal. Since we know the hypotenuse, we can find the other sides of the triangle, which are the sides of the square. As we know, in a 45:45:90 triangle, the ratio of the sides is $x : x : x\sqrt{2}$. Since the diagonal is 5, we know that $x\sqrt{2} = 5$, so the side $x = \frac{5}{\sqrt{2}}$. The area of the square is therefore $\frac{5}{\sqrt{2}} \times \frac{5}{\sqrt{2}} = 12.5$.

12. **B** Let's plug in. If the length of A is $\dfrac{1}{3}$ the length of B, let's make the length of $B = 6$ and the length of $A = 2$. If the width of A is twice the width of B, let's make the width of $B = 4$ and the width of $A = 8$. Now the area of $A = 2 \times 8 = 16$, and the area of B is $6 \times 4 = 24$. $\dfrac{A}{B}$ is $\dfrac{16}{24}$, or $\dfrac{2}{3}$.

BOXES AND CANS

Forget spheres, cones, and other complicated 3-D nightmares. Most often, you will be asked only to deal with rectangular solids (boxes), cubes (square boxes), and possibly cylinders (cans).

No matter what the shape is, the volume equals the area of one face × the third dimension (the depth or the height). Here are the formulas you need to know:

Rectangular Box
Volume $= l \times w \times h$

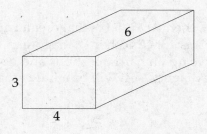

$V = lwh$
$V = 6(3)(4)$
$V = 72$

Cube
Volume $= s^3$

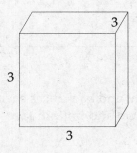

$V = s^3$
$V = 3^3$
$V = 27$

To find the diagonal of a box, draw in two right triangles: one on the end of the box and the other cutting through the box. The second triangle will have the hypotenuse of the first triangle as its base, the length of the box as its height, and the diagonal of the box as its hypotenuse. Here's how it will look:

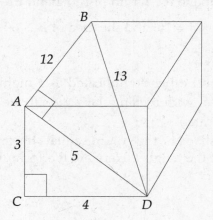

If *AC* is 3 and *DC* is 4, then *AD* is 5 (Pythagorean triple). If *AD* is 5 and *AB* is 12, then *BD* (the diagonal) is 13. (Another Pythagorean triple.) As you can probably guess, this only shows up on hard questions and not that often. You can also estimate the length of the diagonal—it will be a little longer than the longest edge of the box.

SURFACE AREA

The surface area of a box is the sum of the areas of each of the faces.

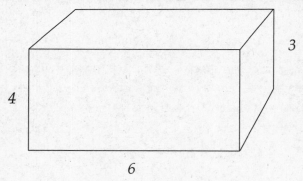

In the figure above, the front and back faces each measure 6 by 4; the side faces each measure 4 by 3; and the top and bottom faces each measure 6 by 3.

Front face $(6 \times 4) = 24$

Back face $(6 \times 4) = 24$

Left face $(4 \times 3) = 12$

Right face $(4 \times 3) = 12$

Top face $(6 \times 3) = 18$

Bottom face $(6 \times 3) = 18$

The surface area is the sum of these faces. $24 + 24 + 12 + 12 + 18 + 18 = 108$.

Cylinder

Volume = $\pi r^2 h$

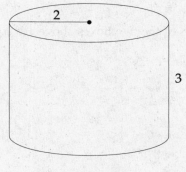

$$V = \pi r^2 h$$
$$V = \pi 2^2 (3)$$
$$V = 12\pi$$

TIP:
If the problem concerns a cone, pyramid, or any shape other than the ones described above, the necessary formula will be given in the question. If you aren't given a formula, you don't need one.

QUICK QUIZ #6

EASY

$V=lwh$

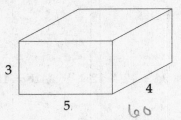

3

4

5

60

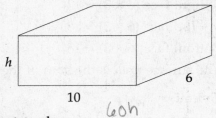

h

10

6

60h

Note: Figures not drawn to scale.

$h=1$

6. If the volumes of the two boxes above are equal, then h equals

(A) 1
(B) 2
(C) 4
(D) 5
(E) 20

MEDIUM

9. Sam is packing toy blocks into a crate. If each block is a cube with a side of 6 inches, and the crate is 1 foot high, 2 feet long, and 2 feet wide, how many blocks can Sam fit into the crate?

(A) 6
(B) 12
(C) 24
(D) 32
(E) 40

2   2

1

$6 = \frac{1}{2} ft$

$\frac{1}{2} \cdot \frac{1}{2} \cdot \frac{1}{2} = \frac{1}{8} ft^3$

$V = 4 ft^3$ $4 / (1/8) = 32$

HARD

12. The surface area of a rectangular solid measuring $5 \times 6 \times 8$ is how much greater than the surface area of a rectangular solid measuring $3 \times 6 \times 8$?

(A) 12
(B) 24
(C) 48
(D) 56
(E) 96

6   3

8

6   5

8

96
+ 80
160
236

48×2
$+ 24 \times 2 =$
18×2

96
48
36
180

Answers and Explanations: Quick Quiz #6

6. **A** The box on the left has volume = $3 \times 4 \times 5 = 60$. The box on the right is then $10 \times 6 \times h = 60$. So $h = 1$. Don't forget to estimate!

9. **D** First draw the crate. It should look like this:

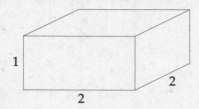

Now visualize putting blocks into the crate. If the blocks are 6 inches high, you'll be able to stack 2 rows in the crate since the crate is a foot high. Now mark off 6-inch intervals along the side of the crate. (You're dividing 2 feet, or 24 inches, by 6 inches.) You can fit 4 blocks along each side. Now multiply everything together and you get $2 \times 4 \times 4 = 32$ blocks.

12. **D** Let's find the surface area of the first figure. It has two sides 5×6, two sides 6×8, and two sides 5×8. Therefore its surface area is $30 + 30 + 48 + 48 + 40 + 40$, which makes 236. The second figure has two sides 3×6, two sides 6×8, and two sides 3×8. Its surface area is $18 + 18 + 48 + 48 + 24 + 24$, or 180. The difference between these two surface areas is 56.

COORDINATE GEOMETRY

Remember how to plot points? The first number is x and the second is y.

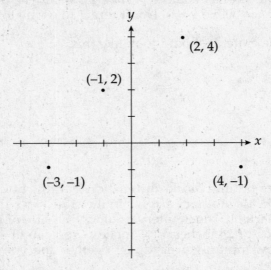

To find the length of a horizontal or vertical line, count the units:

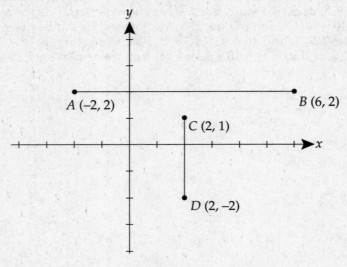

$AB = 8$ and $CD = 3$

To find the length of any other line, draw in a right triangle and use the Pythagorean theorem:

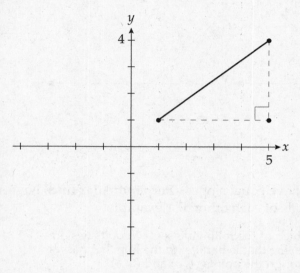

The triangle has legs of 3 and 4, so $3^2 + 4^2 = c^2$, and $c = 5$. (It's a Pythagorean triple again.)

To find the slope, put the rise over the run. The formula is

$$\textbf{slope} = \frac{y_1 - y_2}{x_1 - x_2} \qquad \frac{y}{x} \quad \frac{\Delta y}{\Delta x} \quad \frac{dy}{dx}$$

It doesn't matter which point you begin with, just be consistent.

What is the slope of the line containing points (2, –3) and (4, 3)? $\frac{-3-3}{2-4} = \frac{-6}{-2} = 3$

$$\text{slope} = \frac{-3-3}{2-4} = \frac{-6}{-2} = 3 \text{ or } \frac{3-(-3)}{4-2} = \frac{6}{2} = 3$$

TIP:

A slope that goes from low to high is positive.

A slope that goes from high to low is negative.

A slope that goes straight across is 0.

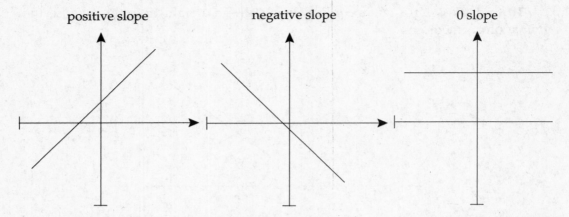

positive slope   negative slope   0 slope

Parallel lines have equal slopes. **Perpendicular lines** have slopes that are negative reciprocals of each other. For example:

> Which of the following sets of points lies on the line that is parallel to the line that passes through the points (1, 3) and (5, 8)?
>
> (A) (–5, –8), (1, 3)
> (B) (12, 2), (8, –3)
> (C) (5, 3), (1,8)
> (D) (15, 3), (6, 2)
> (E) (–7, –5), (2, 3)

First, find the slope of the first set of points.

$$\text{slope} = \frac{3-8}{1-5} = \frac{-5}{-4} = \frac{5}{4}$$

Then check the answer choices and look for the set of points that has an equal slope. The correct answer is (B).

Let's try the same thing with perpendicular lines.

> Which of the following sets of points lies on the line that is perpendicular to the line that passes through the points (1, 3) and (5, 8)?
>
> (A) (16, 7), (11, 11)
> (B) (8, 5), (3, 1)
> (C) (2, 5), (3, 13)
> (D) (7, 8), (5, 11)
> (E) (3, 3), (8, 8)

We already found the slope. Now we need its negative reciprocal, which is $\frac{-4}{5}$. Check the answers. Answer choice (A) gives us:

$$\text{slope} = \frac{7-11}{16-11} = \frac{-4}{5}$$

Bingo!

QUICK QUIZ #7

EASY

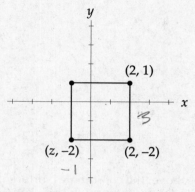

(2, 1)

(z, –2)   (2, –2)

–1

ß

4. If the figure above is a square, what is the value of z?

    (A) –2
    (B) –1
    (C)   1
    (D)   2
    (E)   4

MEDIUM

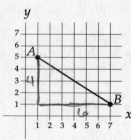

$4^2 + 6^2 = c^2$
$16 + 36 = \sqrt{52}$

14. In the figure above, what is the length of *AB*?

    (A) 4

    (B) $2\sqrt{6}$

    (C) 7

    (D) $\sqrt{52}$

    (E) $\sqrt{63}$

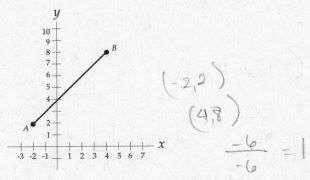

19. In the figure above, the coordinates for point A are $(-2, 2)$ and the coordinates for point B are $(4, 8)$. If line CD, not shown, is parallel to the line AB, what is the slope of line CD?

    (A) −1
    (B)   0
    (C)   1
    (D)   2
    (E)   4

ANSWERS AND EXPLANATIONS: QUICK QUIZ #7

4. **B** Just count the units. Remember that coordinates in the lower left quadrant will always be negative.

14. **D** Use the units to measure each leg. You should get one leg = 4 and the other = 6. Now use the Pythagorean theorem: $4^2 + 6^2 = c^2$.

$$16 + 36 = c^2$$

$$52 = c^2$$

$$\sqrt{52} = c$$

19. **C** Write in the coordinates of A and B. $A = (-2, 2)$ and $B = (4, 8)$. So the slope of $AB = \dfrac{2-8}{-2-4} = \dfrac{-6}{-6} = 1$. If CD is parallel to AB, it has the same slope. (You could draw in a parallel line and recalculate the slope, but you'd be doing extra work.)

CHARTS AND GRAPHS

The key to chart questions is to take a moment to size up the chart before you attack the question. Pay particular attention to what units are used.

Number of Dogs Washed by Deidre's Dog Wash

January	🐕 🐕 🐕 🐕 🐕
February	🐕 🐕
March	🐕 🐕 🐕 🐕 100%
April	🐕 🐕 🐕 🐕 🐕 🐕 🐕
May	🐕 🐕 🐕 🐕 🐕 🐕
June	🐕 🐕 🐕 🐕 🐕 🐕 🐕 🐕

🐕 = 100 dogs

Above is a chart representing how many dogs were washed by Deirdre's Dog Wash in the first half of 2004. Which month features the greatest percent increase of the number of dogs washed over the previous month?

(A) February
(B) March
(C) April
(D) May
(E) June

First, note the units. Each dog shape represents 100 dogs. Now, let's attack the question. We need to find the percent increase, which you'll recall is the difference between two numbers divided by the original number. (A) and (D) both show a decrease in the number of dogs, so eliminate them. In March, 400 dogs were washed, while 200 dogs were washed in the previous month. Using our percent increase formula, we get

$$\frac{\text{difference}}{\text{original}} = \frac{400 - 200}{200} = \frac{200}{200} = 100\%$$

None of the other choices is even close, so (B) is our answer.

If you are asked to identify the **graph of a function**, use the vertical line test. A vertical line drawn through the graph of a function should only cross the graph once. If the line passes through the graph more than once, the graph is not a function.

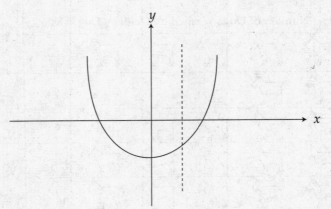

This is the graph of a function; the vertical line only crosses the graph once.

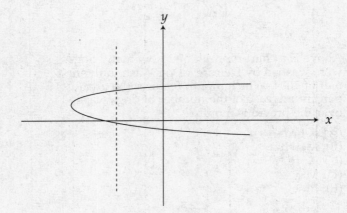

This is NOT the graph of a function. Notice how the vertical line crosses the graph in two places.

To match a graph to a function, plug points from the graph into the function and see if they make the function true. Plug in the x coordinate for the x in the function and the y coordinate in for the $f(x)$.

The **graph of an inequality** will consist of a shaded region marked off with a boundary line. Any points within the shaded region must make the inequality true. Points within the unshaded region will make the inequality false. If you change the inequality sign to an equal sign, any points on the boundary line will make the resultant equation true.

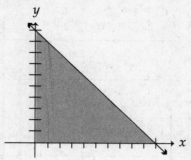

The figure above could represent which of the following?

(A) $|x| + |y| < 10$

(B) $x + y \leq 10$

(C) $x + y = 10$ $y = 10 - x$ $9 = 10 - x$ $-1 = -x$ $1 = x$

(D) $x + y \geq 10$

(E) It cannot be determined from the information given.

Let's plug in some points from the graph and see what happens. (0, 0) is within the shaded region, and it's easy to check, so we'll start there. Plugging in these values for x and y eliminates choice (D). (C) is out as well since (0, 0) does not satisfy this equation. Now let's try something like (−4, 9). Plugging in this to choice (A) shows the inequality to be false, so (A) can't be the answer. The answer is (B).

QUICK QUIZ #8

EASY

Adore-a-Bubble Soda Company's Sales

Flavor	1980	2000
Snappy Apple	50%	50%
Raspberry Rush	25%	5%
Fresh Fizz	10%	12%
Cranberry Crackle	12%	10%
Purple Pop	3%	3%
Total	100%	100%

6. The table above shows the Adore-a-Bubble Soda Company's sales for 1980 and 2000. The company sold 200 trillion cans of soda in 1980. If the company sold 40 trillion more cans of soda in 2000 than it did in 1980, then for which flavor did the <u>number</u> of cans of soda sold increase by 20% from 1980 to 2000?

   (A) Snappy Apple
   (B) Raspberry Rush
   (C) Fresh Fizz
   (D) Cranberry Crackle
   (E) Purple Pop

MEDIUM

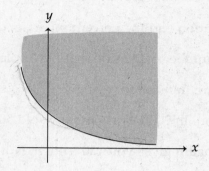

12. The above graph could represent which of the following inequalities?

(A) $y \le \dfrac{1}{x}$

(B) $y < \left(\dfrac{1}{2}\right)^x$

(C) $y \ge \dfrac{1}{x}$

(D) $y \ge \left(\dfrac{1}{2}\right)^x$

(E) $y \ge x^{-\frac{1}{2}}$

HARD

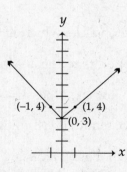

13. If the graph above is that of $f(x)$, which of the following could be $f(x)$?

(A) $f(x) = \dfrac{|x|}{3}$

(B) $f(x) = \left|\dfrac{x}{3}\right|$

(C) $f(x) = |x| + 3$

(D) $f(x) = |x + 3|$

(E) $f(x) = |3x|$

Answers and Explanations: Quick Quiz #8

6. **A** Use percent translation and the percent increase/decrease formula.

   For example, the number of cans of Snappy Apple sold in 1980 is 50% of 200 trillion. Using translation, you get $\frac{50}{100} \times 200$ trillion $= \frac{1}{2} \times 200$ trillion $= 100$ trillion. In 2000, the company sold 50% of 240 trillion. Using translation again gives you 120 trillion. Now you need to find the percent increase using the formula:

$$\text{Percent increase} = \frac{Differences}{Original} \times 100$$

   Plugging in the values you found above gives you

   $\frac{120 \text{ trillion} - 100 \text{ trillion}}{100 \text{ trillion}} \times 100 = \frac{1}{5} \times 100 = 20$. This means that sales of Snappy Apple increased by 20%, so (A) is the correct answer.

12. **D** Since the shading is above the solid curve, y must be greater than or equal to some function of x: eliminate (A) and (B). The equation must be defined at $x = 0$: eliminate (C) and (E).

13. **C** The bar marks are absolute value, which is the distance from zero on a number line. Plug in the points to the answers. Point $(-1, 4)$ means that if x is -1, $f(x)$ is 4. So, for (A), does $4 = \frac{|-1|}{3}$? No, eliminate (A). For (B), does $4 = \frac{|-1|}{3}$? No, eliminate (B). For (C), does $4 = |-1| + 3$? Yes, because $4 = 1 + 3$. Keep (C). For (D), does $4 = |-1 + 3|$? No, eliminate (D). For (E), does $4 = |3(-1)|$? No, eliminate (E). Only (C) remains.

GEOMETRY: FINAL TIPS AND REMINDERS

- Always estimate first when the figure is drawn to scale.

- Always write the information given on the diagram, including any information you figure out along the way.

- If you don't know how to start, just look and see what shapes are involved. The solution to the problem will come through using the information we've gone over that pertains to that shape.

QUICK QUIZ #9

EASY

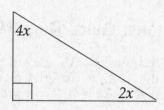

6. In the figure above, $x =$

 (A) 15
 (B) 45
 (C) 85
 (D) 105
 (E) 125

MEDIUM

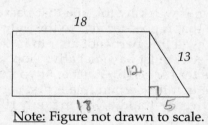

Note: Figure not drawn to scale.

11. The figure above is composed of a rectangle and a triangle. What is the perimeter of the figure above?

 (A) 49
 (B) 66
 (C) 70
 (D) 93
 (E) 111

HARD

14. What is the slope of a line that is perpendicular to the line that passes through points (1, 2) and (2, 4)?

(A) -2

(B) $-\dfrac{1}{2}$

(C) 1

(D) $\dfrac{1}{2}$

(E) 2

$$\frac{-2}{-1} = 2$$

$$-\frac{1}{2}$$

ANSWERS AND EXPLANATIONS: QUICK QUIZ #9

6. **A** Since the angles in a triangle always add up to 180, and we have a right angle, we know that the other two angles must have a sum of 90. We can write the equation: $4x + 2x = 90$. Now we can solve $6x = 90$, so x must be equal to 15.

11. **B** If you remember the ratios that work for the Pythagorean theorem, you'll remember that 5:12:13 is one common set of sides for right triangles on the SAT. Since this right triangle has sides 5 and 13, we know that the height of the triangle (which is also the height of the rectangle) is 12. So to figure out the perimeter of the whole figure, we need to add up the sides: $18 + 12 + 18 + 5 + 13 = 66$.

14. **B** Let's start by estimating. If we draw the line that passes through (1, 2) and (2, 4), we see that it goes up and to the right, so it has a positive slope. If we draw a line perpendicular to it, the new line will go down and to the right, so it must have negative slope. This means that the answer has to be either (A) or (B). Further, if you drew your diagram accurately, you'll notice that the second line is at a very shallow angle, so its slope must be between -1 and 0, leaving only (B) as the possible answer choice.

5

Grid-In Questions

GRID-INS

Grid-in questions have no answer choices. You must solve the question, write your answer on a grid, and bubble it in. This isn't as bad as it sounds. The order of difficulty applies, so the first three questions (11–13) are easy, the middle four questions (14–17) are medium, and the final three questions (18–20) are hard. Take your time on the easy and medium questions, as always.

TIPS FOR GRID-IN HAPPINESS

- Don't bother to reduce fractions: $\frac{3}{6}$ is as good as $\frac{1}{2}$.

- Don't round off decimals. If your answer has more than four digits, just start to the left of the decimal point and fit in as many as you can.

- Don't grid in mixed fractions. Either convert to one fraction or a decimal. (Use 4.25 or $\frac{17}{4}$, not $4\frac{1}{4}$.)

- If the question asks for "one possible value," any answer that works is okay.

- Forget about negatives, variables, π, \$, and %. You can't grid 'em.

- You can still plug in if the question has an implied variable.

QUICK QUIZ #1

EASY

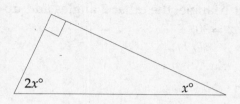

11. What is the value of x?

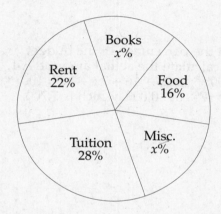

MEDIUM

15. The chart above shows Orwell's projected expenditures for his freshman year at River State University. If he plans to spend a total of $10,000 for the year, how many dollars will Orwell spend on books?

HARD

19. At a certain university, the ratio of science majors to art majors was 3:1. If 600 other students changed their majors to science and art in a ratio of 1:2, the new ratio of science to art majors is 4:3. What was the original number of art majors?

Answers and Explanations: Quick Quiz #1

11. **30**

    Since this is a right triangle, the other 2 angles add up to 90. So $3x = 90$ and $x = 30$.

15. **1700**

    Two steps: First figure out the percentage of the budget spent on books, and then calculate the actual amount. All the pie slices add up to 100%, so $28 + 16 + 22 + 2x = 100$. $2x = 34$ and $x = 17\%$. Take 17% of 10,000, which is 1,700.

19. **200**

    Write out the ratio so you can see what you're doing:

    S:A

    3:1

    If we're adding in 600 students in a ratio of 1:2, figure out the actual numbers of each by adding the parts in the ratio $(1 + 2 = 3)$ and dividing that sum into the total $(600 ÷ 3 = 200)$. Now multiply that quotient by the parts in the ratio: $200 × 1 = 200$ and $200 × 2 = 400$. So out of 600 students, 200 are added to science and 400 are added to art:

    S:A

    3:1

    + 200:400

    4:3

    The easiest thing to do next is to plug in numbers for the original ratio of 3:1. Since we're dealing in hundreds, let's try 300:100. With the new students added in, we get 500:500, or 1:1. We need to try something bigger, like 600:200 (still maintaining our original 3:1 ratio). Add in the new students, and you get 800:600, or 4:3. So the number of original art majors was 200.

6

Problem Sets

The following groups of questions were designed for quick, concentrated study. The problems come in groups of ten (three easy, four medium, three hard). Answers and explanations follow immediately. The idea is for you to check your answers right after working the problems so that you can learn from your mistakes before you continue.

Don't simply count up how many you got wrong and then breeze on to the next thing—take a careful look at *how* you got the question wrong. Did you use the wrong strategy? Not remember the necessary basic math? Make a goofy computation error? Write an equation and plug in at the same time?

You need to know the cause of your mistakes before you can stop making them.

We put together sets of plugging in, geometry, exponent, and other typical problem types to help you learn how to recognize those types of questions when they come up—so pay attention to the look and feel of them. For these strategy questions, we put the answers and explanations right after each level of difficulty, so you can be certain of mastering the strategy before going on to more difficult questions. When you get to Problem Set 6, the answers to all the questions in the set will follow the set immediately.

One last thing—the question numbers correspond exactly to the difficulty level. For the 20-question multiple-choice section, the easy questions are number 1 to 8, the mediums are number 7 to 14, and the hard ones are number 15 to 20. We point this out because you must always be aware of the difficulty level of the question you're working on.

PROBLEM SET 1: PLUGGING IN

EASY

1. Sinéad has 4 more than three times the number of hats that Maria has. If Maria has x hats, then in terms of x, how many hats does Sinéad have?

   (A) $3x + 4$
   (B) $3(x + 4)$
   (C) $4(x + 3)$
   (D) $4(3x)$
   (E) $7x$

2. When 6 is subtracted from $10p$, the result is t. Which of the following equations represents the statement above?

   (A) $t = 6(p - 10)$
   (B) $t = 6p - 10$
   (C) $t = 10(6 - p)$
   (D) $10p - 6 = t$
   (E) $10 - 6p = t$

3. Sally scored a total of $4b + 12$ points in a certain basketball game. She scored the same number of points in each of the game's 4 periods. In terms of b, how many points did she score in each period?

   (A) $b - 8$
   (B) $b + 3$
   (C) $b + 12$
   (D) $4b + 3$
   (E) $16b + 48$

MEDIUM

t = 3　　*x = 4*

4. If *t* is a prime number, and *x* is a factor of 12, then $\frac{t}{x}$ could be all of the following EXCEPT

$\frac{3}{4}$

I is not a prime # !!

(A) $\frac{1}{12}$

(B) $\frac{1}{4}$

(C) $\frac{1}{2}$

(D) 1

(E) 2

5. Roseanne is 6 years younger than Tom will be in 2 years. Roseanne is now *x* years old. In terms of *x*, how old was Tom 3 years ago?

x = 10

In 2 years　Tom = 16

TOM = 14

Tom was = 11

(A) *x* – 7
(B) *x* – 1
(C) *x* + 1
(D) *x* + 3
(E) *x* + 5

6. A phone company charges 10 cents per minute for the first 3 minutes of a call and 10 – *c* cents for each minute thereafter. What is the cost, in cents, of a 10-minute phone call?

C = 3

(A) 200 – 20*c*
(B) 100*c* + 70
(C) 30 + 7*c*
(D) 100 – 7*c*
(E) 100 – 70*c*

30　49
3　7
79

7. If $0 < pt < 1$, and *p* is a negative integer, which of the following must be less than –1?

$p = -1$　　$t = -\frac{1}{2}$

(A) *p*

(B) *p* – *t*

(C) *t* + *p*

(D) 2*t*

(E) $t \times \frac{1}{2}$

8. If x and y are positive integers, and
   $\sqrt{x} = y + 3$, then $y^2 =$

   (A) $x - 9$
   (B) $x + 9$
   (C) $x^2 - 9$
   (D) $x - 6\sqrt{x} + 9$
   (E) $x^2 - 6\sqrt{x} + 9$

   Handwritten: $x - 1$
   $(\sqrt{x} - 3)^2 = (y)^2$

   $(\sqrt{x} - 3)(\sqrt{x} - 3)$

   $x - 3\sqrt{x} - 3\sqrt{x} + 9$

   $x - 6\sqrt{x} + 9$

9. If cupcakes are on sale at 8 for c cents, and gingerbread squares are on sale at 6 for g cents, what is the cost, in cents, of 2 cupcakes and 1 gingerbread square?

   (A) $8c + 3g$

   (B) $\dfrac{cg}{3}$

   (C) $\dfrac{8c + 6g}{3}$

   (D) $\dfrac{8c + 3g}{14}$

   (E) $\dfrac{3c + 2g}{12}$

   Handwritten:
   $8 = c \qquad 8 = 80$
   $6 = g \qquad 6 = 60$
   $c = 80$
   $g = 60$

   $\dfrac{8}{80} = \dfrac{2}{x}$

   $160 = 8c \qquad c = 20$

   $\dfrac{6}{60} = \dfrac{1}{g}$

   $60 = 6g \qquad g = 10$

   30 cents

10. If the side of a square is $x + 1$, then the diagonal of the square is

    (A) $x^2 + 1$
    (B) $2x + 2$
    (C) $x\sqrt{2} + \sqrt{2}$
    (D) $x^2 + 2$
    (E) $\sqrt{2x} + \sqrt{2}$

    Handwritten: $x = 2$

    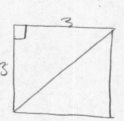

    $3^2 + 3^2 = c^2$
    $\sqrt{18}$
    $3\sqrt{2}$

ANSWERS AND EXPLANATIONS: PROBLEM SET 1

EASY

1. **A** Forget the algebra. Let's plug in 2 for x, so Maria has 2 hats. Triple that number is 6. Sinéad has 4 more than triple, so Sinéad has $4 + 6 = 10$. You should put a circle around 10, so you can remember it's the answer to the question, the magic number. Now plug 2 into the answer choices. (A) gives us $3(2) + 4 = 10$, which is just what we're looking for.

2. **D** Plug in 2 for p. $2 \times 10 = 20$; $20 - 6 = 14$. So $t = 14$. (Since this is an equation, when you pick one number, the other number is automatically produced by the equation.) If $p = 2$ and $t = 14$, (A) is $14 = 6(2 - 10)$. Does $14 = 12 - 60$? Not on this planet. (D) is $10(2) - 6 = 14$, or $20 - 6 = 14$. The equation works, so that's our answer.

3. **B** Maybe Sally should try out for the WNBA. Let's make $b = 2$. That means she scored $4(2) + 12 = 20$ points total. If she scored the same number of points in each of the 4 periods, we have to divide the total by 4, so she scored $20 \div 4 = 5$ points per period. Put a circle around 5. Now on to the answer choices. (A) is $2 - 8$. (B) is $2 + 3 = 5$, which is our magic number.

> **TIP:**
>
> Notice how we keep plugging in 2? That's because we're trying to make things as easy as possible. To get these questions right, you didn't *have* to pick 2; on some questions, 2 might not work so well. You can pick whatever you want. Just make sure your number doesn't require you to make ugly, unpleasant calculations. *Avoiding hard work* is the name of the game. If the number you pick turns bad on you, pick another one.

Medium

4. **A** This question is tricky to spot as a plugging in question because the answer choices don't have variables. Just remember that most of the time you can make things easier by plugging in numbers for variables in the question. Here we go: Make a short list of possibilities for t, starting with the first prime number. Then do the same for x, listing the factors of 12 in pairs.

$$t = 2, 3, 5, 7 \qquad\qquad x = 1, 12, 2, 6, 3, 4$$

The question asks us for $\dfrac{t}{x}$, which we can make by putting any number in our t column over any number from our x column. (B) is $\dfrac{3}{12}$. (C) is $\dfrac{3}{6}$. (D) is $\dfrac{2}{2}$. (E) is $\dfrac{2}{1}$. No matter what we do, we can't make $\dfrac{1}{12}$, so A is our answer. If you didn't remember that 1 is not prime, you were probably banging your head against a wall. When that happens, go on to the next question.

5. **C** Let $x = 10$, so Roseanne is now 10 years old. That's 6 years younger than 16, so Tom must be 16 in 2 years, which makes him 14 now. The question asks for Tom's age 3 years ago; if he's 14 now, 3 years ago he was 11. Circle 11. In the answer choices, plug 10 in for x. (A) is $10 - 3$. Nope. (B) is $10 - 1$. Nope. (C) is $10 + 1$. Yeah!

6. **D** Let $c = 8$. The first 3 minutes of the call would be $3(10)$, or 30 cents. The remaining minutes would be charged at $10 - 8$ cents, or 2 cents a minute. There are 7 minutes remaining, so $2 \times 7 = 14$. The total cost is $30 + 14 = 44$ cents. On to the answer choices: (A) and (B) are way too big. (C) is $30 + 7(8) = 86$. (D) is $100 - 56 = 44$. Bingo.

7. **C** First take a good look at $0 < pt < 1$. We know that pt is a positive

fraction. If p is a negative integer, then t must be a negative fraction.

Now we're ready to plug in. (Or you can just try numbers until you find

some that satisfy the inequality.) Let $p = -1$ and $t = -\dfrac{1}{2}$. Try them in the

answer choices, crossing out any answer that's –1 or higher. (A) is –1,

cross it out. (B) is $-\dfrac{1}{2}$, cross it out. (C) is $-1\dfrac{1}{2}$, leave it in. (D) is –1, cross

it out. (E) is –1, cross it out. The trouble with *must be* questions is that

you can only *eliminate* answers by plugging in, you can't simply choose

the first answer that works. That's because the answer may work with

certain numbers but not with others—and you're looking for an answer

that *must be true*, no matter what numbers you pick. These questions can

be time-consuming, so if you're running low on time, you may want to

skip them.

HARD

8. **D** Let $x = 25$. That makes $y = 2$. The question asks for y^2, and $2^2 = 4$. Circle

it. Now try the answer choices. (A) is $25 - 9$. (B) is $25 + 9$. (C) is huge.

(D) is $25 - 30 + 9 = 4$. Not so bad, huh?

9. **E** Let $c = 16$ and $g = 12$. That means the cupcakes and the gingerbread

squares sell for 2 cents apiece. One gingerbread square and two

cupcakes will cost 6 cents. Circle 6. On to the answer choices, plugging

in 16 for c and 12 for g. (E) gives you $\dfrac{3(16) + 2(12)}{12} = 6$. Use your

calculator for that last part. Get it right? Then go to a bakery and

celebrate.

10. **C** Draw yourself a little square and label the sides $x + 1$. Draw in a

diagonal. Let $x = 2$. The side of the square is then 3, and the diagonal is

$3\sqrt{2}$. (The diagonal is the hypotenuse of a 45:45:90 triangle.) Plug 2 into

the answer choices. (C) gives you $2\sqrt{2} + \sqrt{2} = 3\sqrt{2}$.

PROBLEM SET 2: MORE PLUGGING IN

EASY

1. Jim and Pam bought x quarts of ice cream for a party. If 10 people attended the party, including Jim and Pam, and if each person ate the same amount of ice cream, which of the following represents the amount of ice cream, in quarts, eaten by each person at the party?

   (A) $10x$

   (B) $5x$

   (C) x

   (D) $\dfrac{x}{5}$

   (E) $\dfrac{x}{10}$

2. If x and y are integers and $\dfrac{x}{y} = 1$, then $x + y$ must be

   (A) positive
   (B) negative
   (C) odd
   (D) even
   (E) greater than 1

3. If $3x - y = 12$, then $\dfrac{y}{3} =$

   (A) $x - 3$
   (B) $x - 4$
   (C) $3x - 4$
   (D) $9x - 12$
   (E) $3x + 4$

MEDIUM

4. When x is divided by 3, the remainder is z. In terms of z, which of the following could be equal to x?

    (A) $z - 3$
    (B) $3 - z$
    (C) $3z$
    (D) $6 + z$
    (E) $9 + 2z$

$$\times X = 8 = 2$$
$$\frac{8}{3} \qquad 3\overline{\smash{)}8} \quad \begin{array}{c} R.1 = Z \\ 1 = Z \end{array}$$
$$\qquad \frac{-6}{2} = R = Z$$

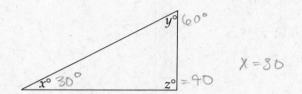

$y° \quad 60°$
$x° \quad 30°$
$z° = 90$
$X = 80$

5. In the figure above, $2x = y$. In terms of x, $z = 90$

    (A) $180 + 2x$
    (B) $180 + x$
    (C) $180 - x$
    (D) $180 - 3x$
    (E) $180 - 4x$

6. If w, x, y, and z are consecutive positive integers, and $w > x > y > z$, which of the following CANNOT be true?

    (A) $x + z = w \qquad 4 > 3 > 2 > 1$
    (B) $y + z = x$
    (C) $x - y = z \qquad w \quad x \quad y \quad z$
    (D) $w - x = y \qquad 10 > 9 > 8 > 7$
    (E) $w - z = y \qquad 5 > 4 > 3 > 2$

7. The volume of a certain rectangular solid is $12x$. If the dimensions of the solid are the integers x, y, and z, what is the greatest possible value of z?

    (A) 36
    (B) 24
    (C) 12
    (D) 6
    (E) 4

$X = 2 \quad V = 24$

$y = 3$

$4y + 4(6) + 2y6 = 24$
$24 + 16y = 24$

$\begin{array}{r} 4 \\ 4z \\ + 2z \\ \hline 24 \end{array}$
$4 + 6z = 24$
$6z = 20$
$z = 20/0$

$2 + 4z + z = 24$
$5z = 22$
$z = 4.4$

$\begin{array}{r} 2xy \\ 2xz \\ + 2yz \\ \hline 24 \end{array}$
$\begin{array}{r} 2(2)y \\ 2(2)z \\ + 2(y)z \\ \hline 24 \end{array}$
$\begin{array}{r} 4y \\ 4z \\ + 2yz \\ \hline 24 \end{array}$
$\begin{array}{r} 12 \\ 4z \\ + 6z \\ \hline 24 \end{array}$

$12 + 10z = 24$
$10z = 24$
$z = 24/0 = 2.4$

HARD

8. If $x^3 < 0 < xy^2z$, which of the following must be true?

    I. xyz is positive
    II. $x^2y^2z^3$ is positive
    III. $x^3y^2z^3$ is positive

    (A) I only
    (B) III only
    (C) I and II only
    (D) II and III only
    (E) I, II, and III

Handwritten: $x = -1$, $y = -2$, $z = -3$, $x^3 = -1$, $xy^2z = 12$

9. When a is divided by 7, the remainder is 4. When b is divided by 3, the remainder is 2. If $0 < a < 24$ and $2 < b < 8$, which of the following could have a remainder of 0 when divided by 8?

    (A) $\dfrac{a}{b}$

    (B) $\dfrac{b}{a}$

    (C) $a - b$

    (D) $a + b$

    (E) ab

Handwritten: $a = 11$, $b = 5$

10. If $3x$, $\dfrac{3}{x}$, and $\dfrac{15}{x}$ are integers, which of the following must also be an integer?

    I. $\dfrac{x}{3}$
    II. x
    III. $6x$

    (A) I only
    (B) II only
    (C) III only
    (D) I and III only
    (E) II and III only

Handwritten: $x = 1$, $x = 3$, $x = \frac{1}{2}$

ANSWERS AND EXPLANATIONS: PROBLEM SET 2

EASY

1. **E** Plug in 20 for x. If 10 people eat 20 quarts, and they all eat the same amount, then each person eats 2 quarts. (The pigs!) Put a circle around 2. Go to the answers and remember that $x = 20$. (A) $= 10 \times 10 = 100$. Nope. (E) $= \dfrac{20}{10} = 2$. Yep.

2. **D** Plug in 2 for x and 2 for y. That satisfies the equation $\dfrac{x}{y} = 1$, and makes $x + y = 4$. Eliminate (B) and (C). How about $-2 = x$ and $-2 = y$? That makes $x + y = -4$. Eliminate (A) and (E).

3. **B** Plug in 5 for x, which makes $y = 3$. So $\dfrac{y}{3} = \dfrac{3}{3} = 1$. Circle 1. On to the answers, and plug in $x = 5$. (A) $= 5 - 3 = 2$. No good. (B) $= 5 - 4 = 1$. There you go.

> **TIP:**
>
> Why do we keep saying "circle it" in the explanations? Because that's the arithmetic answer to the question. All that's left to do is plug in for the variables in the answer choices, and look for your circled number. We tell you to circle that number so it won't get lost in the shuffle, and you can keep track of what you're doing.
>
> Notice how sometimes, as in question 2, you may have to plug in more than one set of numbers. That doesn't mean you're doing anything wrong, it's just the nature of the question—and it tends to happen on *must be* questions.
>
> Also remember that you are trying to find numbers to plug in that make getting an answer to the question easy—so in question 3, if we'd plugged in $x = 2$, that would've made y negative. Who wants to deal with negatives if they don't have to? If some kind of nastiness happens, bail out and *pick new numbers*.

MEDIUM

4. **D** Let $x = 7$ so $z = 1$. Try the answers. (D) is $6 + z$, or $6 + 1 = 7$. No sweat.

5. **D** Plug in 10 for x, which makes $y = 20$. Remember that a triangle has 180°, so the third angle, z, must equal $180 - 30 = 150$. Circle 150. Try the answers, with $x = 10$. (D) gives us $180 - 30 = 150$.

6. **D** First put the inequalities in order: $w > x > y > z$. Plug in consecutive positive numbers for the variables: $w = 5$, $x = 4$, $y = 3$, $z = 2$. Now try the answers.

        (A) $4 + 2 = 5$. No, so leave it in.

        (B) $3 + 2 = 4$. No, so leave it in.

        (C) $4 - 3 = 2$. No, so leave it in.

        (D) $5 - 4 = 3$. No, so leave it in.

        (E) $5 - 2 = 3$. Yes, so cross it out.

Whew. We didn't have very good luck. Let's try a new set of numbers. $w = 4$, $x = 3$, $y = 2$, and $z = 1$. This time (A), (B), and (C) all work, so we get rid of 'em—that leaves (D) as our answer. Watch out when the question says CANNOT; it's all too easy to get mixed up and start thinking in the wrong direction. Look for answers that *work* and cross them out, rather than looking for the answer that *doesn't* work.

7. **C** First, draw yourself a picture. (Think shoebox.) Plug in 2 for x. The formula for volume of a rectangular solid is length × width × height—in this case, xyz. Our volume is $12x = 12(2) = 24$. Let's come up with 3 different numbers—2 is one of them—that give us 24 when multiplied together.

A chart is never a bad idea. It keeps you organized.

x	y	z
2	1	12

Since y is as low as possible, z is as big as possible. Go with it. If you're not convinced, try other combinations—but don't forget, the question asks for the greatest possible value of z.

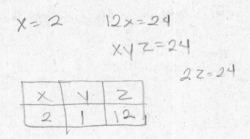

HARD

8. **B** Since we've got a lot of exponents, we want to plug in the smallest numbers we can. Positive/negative is what this question is about. Let's take it part by part. If $x^3 < 0$, we know x must be negative: Let $x = -1$. If $-1(y^2z)$ is positive, let $z = -2$. Beware! We don't know whether y is positive or negative, so we can't plug in anything for it. Let's look at I, II, and III, and remember we're looking for something that *must be* true:

   I. $xyz = -1(y)(-2)$. Maybe it's positive and maybe it isn't. It depends on the sign of y. And we don't know the sign of y.

   II. $x^2y^2z = 1(y^2)(-2)$. Sorry. It's negative.

   III. $x^3y^2z^3 = 1(y^2)(-2^3)$. Well, well, well. Since y is squared, it has to be positive. And the product of the other two negatives equals positive. It works.

9. **D** Plug in 11 for a and 5 for b. Those two choices satisfy all the conditions of the problem. Check the answers: (A) and (B) are fractions, forget about 'em. (C) is $11 - 5 = 6$, which isn't divisible by 8. (D) gives you $11 + 5 = 16$. If we divide 16 by 8, we get a quotient of 2 and a remainder of 0. End of story.

10. **C** How about plugging in 3 for x? Try the answers—we're looking for integers, so if the answer isn't an integer, we can cross it out.

   I. $\dfrac{x}{3} = \dfrac{3}{3} = 1$ OK so far.

   II. $x = 3$ OK so far.

   III. $6x = 6 \cdot 3 = 18$.   OK so far.

At this point, your average test taker figures the question is pretty easy and picks (E). Not you, my friend. *This is a hard question.* You must go an extra step. Plug in a new number. Since the question concerns integers, what if we plug in something that isn't an integer? Like $x = \dfrac{1}{3}$?

   I. $\dfrac{\frac{1}{3}}{3} = \dfrac{1}{9}$. That's no integer. Cross it out.

   II. $\dfrac{1}{3}$. No good either.

   III. $6\left(\dfrac{1}{3}\right) = 2$. Okay.

Since we have eliminated I and II, only III remains.

PROBLEM SET 3: PLUGGING IN THE ANSWER CHOICES

EASY

1. If x is a positive integer, and $x + 12 = x^2$, what is the value of x?

   $4 + 12 = 16$
   $6 + 12 = 18$

   (A) 2
   (B) 4
   (C) 6
   (D) 8
   (E) 12

2. If twice the sum of three consecutive numbers is 12, and the two lowest numbers add up to 3, what is the highest number?

   (A) 2
   (B) 3
   (C) 6
   (D) 9
   (E) 12

   $2(x+y+z) = 12$ $2(x+3) = 12$
   $y + z = 3$ $x + 3 = 6$
                              $x = 3$

3. If $2^x = 8^{(x-4)}$, then $x =$

   (A) 4
   (B) 6
   (C) 8 $256 =$
   (D) 9
   (E) 64

MEDIUM

4. If Jane bought 3 equally priced shirts on sale, she would have 2 dollars left over. If instead she bought 10 equally priced pairs of socks, she would have 7 dollars left over. If the prices of both shirts and socks are integers, which of the following, in dollars, could be the amount that Jane has to spend?

   $3x + 2$

   $10y + 7$

   (A) 28
   (B) 32
   (C) 47
   (D) 57
   (E) 60

5. During a vacation together, Bob spent twice as much as Josh, who spent four times as much as Ralph. If Bob and Ralph together spent $180, how much did Josh spend?

   (A) $20
   (B) $80
   (C) $120
   (D) $160
   (E) $180

6. Tina has half as many marbles as Louise. If Louise gave away 3 of her marbles and lost 2 more, she would have 1 more marble than Tina. How many marbles does Tina have?

   (A) 2
   (B) 3
   (C) 5
   (D) 6
   (E) 7

7. In a bag of jellybeans, $\frac{1}{3}$ are cherry and $\frac{1}{4}$ are licorice. If the remaining 20 jellybeans are orange, how many jellybeans are in the bag?

   (A) 12
   (B) 16
   (C) 32
   (D) 36
   (E) 48

Hard

8. If the circumference of a circle is equal to twice its area, then the area of the circle equals

   (A) 2
   (B) π
   (C) 2π
   (D) 4π
   (E) 16π

9. If $r = \dfrac{6}{3s + 2}$ and $tr = \dfrac{2}{3s + 2}$, then $t =$

    (A) $\dfrac{1}{4}$

    (B) $\dfrac{1}{3}$

    (C) 2

    (D) 3

    (E) 4

10. If x^2 is added to $\dfrac{5}{4y}$, the sum is $\dfrac{5+y}{4y}$. If y is a positive integer, which of the following is the value of x?

    (A) $\dfrac{1}{4}$

    (B) $\dfrac{1}{2}$

    (C) $\dfrac{4}{5}$

    (D) 1

    (E) 5

$$x^2 + \dfrac{5}{4y} = \dfrac{5+y}{4y} \qquad y = 1$$

$$x^2 + \dfrac{5}{4} = \dfrac{6}{4}$$

Answers and Explanations: Problem Set 3

Easy

1. **B** Start with (C) 6 = x. That gives you 6 + 12 = 36. No good. At this point, don't stare at the other choices, waiting for divine inspiration—just pick another one and try it. It's okay if the next answer you try isn't right either. If we plug in 4 for x, we get 4 + 12 = 16. The equation works, so that's that.

2. **B** Start with (C). If the highest number is 6, the other two are 5 and 4. 5 and 4 don't add up to 3—cross out (C). Try (B). If the highest number is 3, the other two numbers are 1 and 2. (They have to be consecutive.) The sum of 3 + 2 + 1= 6, and twice the sum of 6 = 12. If you picked (A), you didn't pay attention to what the question asked for. Be sure to reread the question so you know which number they want.

3. **B** Try (C) first. Does $2^8 = 8^4$? Nope. (Use your calculator.) Try something lower, like (B). Does $2^6 = 8^2$? Yessiree.

Medium

4. **C** Try (C) first. If Jane has $47 to spend, 47 ÷ 3 = 15 with 2 left over. (The shirts cost $15 apiece.) Now try 47 ÷ 10 = 4, with 7 left over. (Socks are $4 a pair.) It works.

5. **B** Try (C) first. If Josh spent $120, Bob spent $240 and Ralph spent $40. That means Bob and Ralph together spent $280, not $180 as the problem tells us. (C) is no good. Since our number is way too big, let's try something smaller. If Josh spent $80, Bob spent $160 and Ralph spent $20. So Bob and Ralph together spent $180. That's more like it.

6. **D** Start with (C). If Tina has 5 marbles, then Louise has 10. If Louise gives away 3, then she has 7. If she loses 2 more, she's down to 5. We're supposed to end up with Louise having 1 more than Tina, but they both have 5. Cross out (C)—and you know you're close to the right answer. Try (D) If Tina has 6, Louise has 12. If Louise gives away and loses 5, she's got 7, which is 1 more than Tina has.

7. **E** Try (C) first. Oops—$\frac{1}{3}$ of 32 is a fraction. Forget (C). Try (D): $\frac{1}{3}$ of 36 = 12. $\frac{1}{4}$ of 36 = 9. Does 12 + 9 + 20 = 36? No. Try (E). $\frac{1}{3}$ of 48 = 16. $\frac{1}{4}$ of 48 = 12. Does 16 + 12 + 20 = 48? Yes!

Making a simple chart will help you keep track of your work:

	D	E
cherry	12	16
licorice	9	12
orange	20	20
TOTAL	41	48

HARD

8. **B** Try (C) first. If the area is 2π, then the radius becomes a fraction. That's probably not going to be the answer, so you should move on. Try (B). If the area is π, then the radius is 1. ($\pi r^2 = \pi$, $r^2 = 1$, $r = 1$.) If $r = 1$, the circumference is $2\pi(1) = 2\pi$. So the circumference is twice the area. Beautiful.

9. **B** Try (C) first. If $t = 2$, then look at the second equation:

$$2r = \frac{2}{3s+2}$$

$$r = \frac{2}{3s+2} \cdot \frac{1}{2}$$

$$r = \frac{1}{3s+2}$$

Compare that to the first equation. No good. Try (B). If $t = \dfrac{1}{3}$, then

$$\frac{r}{3} = 2(3s+2)$$

$$r = \frac{2}{3s+2} \cdot 3$$

$$r = \frac{6}{3s+2}$$

Same as the first equation. You're done. Whew.

10. **B** Choice (C) is particularly nasty here, so let's ignore it. Try Choice (D), plugging in 1 for x. You get $1 + \dfrac{5}{4y} = \dfrac{5+y}{4y}$ or $1 = \dfrac{1}{4}$. (The y drops out.) (B) gives you $\dfrac{1}{4} + \dfrac{5}{4y} = \dfrac{5+y}{4y}$ or $\dfrac{1}{4} = \dfrac{1}{4}$. You could also solve by plugging in—choose a positive integer for y, plug it into the equation, and see what happens. You end up with $x = \dfrac{1}{2}$.

> **TIP:**
> When you're plugging in, start with (C) unless (C) is hard to work with, as in question 10. In that case, try the integers, since they'll be easier to do anyway. And don't worry if you have to try a couple of answer choices before you hit the right one—the first one you do is always the slowest, because you're still finding your way. Subsequent tries should be easier. And plugging in is always easier than writing equations.

PROBLEM SET 4: MORE PLUGGING IN THE ANSWER CHOICES

Easy

1. If $\dfrac{a-4}{28} = \dfrac{1}{4}$, then $a =$

   (A) 11 $\dfrac{3}{28}$

   (B) 10

   (C) 7 $\dfrac{a-4}{28} = \dfrac{1}{4}$

   (D) 6 $4(a-4) = 28$

   (E) $\dfrac{3}{28}$ $a-4 = 7$

                    $a = 11$

2. If the area of $\triangle ABC$ is 21, and the length of the height minus the length of the base equals 1, then the base of the triangle is equal to

   (A) 1

   (B) 2

   (C) 4

   (D) 6

   (E) 7

   $h - b = 1$

   $\frac{1}{2}bh = 21$

   $h = 7 \quad b = 6$

3. If $d^2 = \sqrt{4} + d + 10$, then $d =$

   (A) –2 $d^2 = d + 12$

   (B) 2

   (C) 3

   (D) 4

   (E) 16

Medium

4. If $\dfrac{4}{x-1} = \dfrac{x+1}{2}$, which of the following is a possible value of x?

   (A) –1

   (B) 0

   (C) 1

   (D) 2

   (E) 3

5. The product of the digits of a two-digit number is 6. If the tens digit is subtracted from the units digit, the result is 5. What is the two-digit number?

(A) 61
(B) 32
(C) 27
(D) 23
(E) 16

(handwritten: tens, xy — units, $x * y = 6$, $x - y = 5$)

6. If $16,000 = 400(x + 9)$, what is the value of x?

(A) 391
(B) 310
(C) 40
(D) 31
(E) 4

7. What is the radius of a circle with an area of $\frac{\pi}{4}$?

(A) 0.2
(B) 0.4
(C) 0.5
(D) 2
(E) 4

(handwritten: $A = \pi r^2$; $\frac{\pi}{4} = \pi r^2$; $\sqrt{\frac{1}{4}} = r$)

HARD

8. If 20 percent of x is 36 less than x percent of $x - 70$, what is the value of x?

(A) 140
(B) 120
(C) 110
(D) 100
(E) 50

(handwritten: $.20x = .x(x-70) - 36$; $22 =$; $28 =$; $29 =$)

9. If $x^2 = y^3$ and $(x - y)^2 = 2x$, then y could equal

(A) 64
(B) 16
(C) 8
(D) 4
(E) 2

(handwritten: $x^2 = 4096$ $(x-16)^2 = 2x$; 64; 4; $x = 8$ $(8-4)^2 = 16$; $y = 4$)

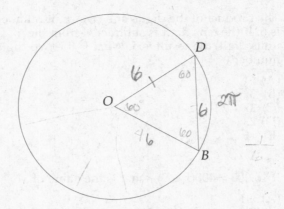

10. In the figure above, $OD = DB$ and arc $DB = 2\pi$. What is the area of the circle?

(A) 64π
(B) 36π
(C) 16π
(D) 12π
(E) 4π

$16\pi = \pi r^2$
$r = 4$
$36\pi = \pi r^2$
$r = 6$

ANSWERS AND EXPLANATIONS: PROBLEM SET 4

EASY

1. **A** Try (C) first. Does $\dfrac{3}{28} = \dfrac{1}{4}$? Nope. Look for a bigger number—(B) gives us $\dfrac{6}{28}$, which is closer, but still no cigar. Choice (A) gives us $\dfrac{7}{28} = \dfrac{1}{4}$.

2. **D** Try (C) first. If the base = 4, then $h - 4 = 1$ and $h = 5$. The formula for area of a triangle is $\dfrac{1}{2}bh$, so the area would be 10. Too small. Try (D). If the base is 6, then $h - 6 = 1$ and $h = 7$. The area is $\dfrac{42}{2} = 21$. Bingo. If you couldn't do this question without looking up the formula for the area of a triangle, that should tell you something.

3. **D** Yes, it looks nasty, but it's a breeze with the miracle of plugging in the answer choices. As always, try (C) first: $3^2 = \sqrt{4} + 3 + 10$; $9 = 2 + 13$. Forget it. Try (D). $4^2 = 2 + 4 + 10$; $16 = 16$. That's it.

MEDIUM

4. **E** Try (C) first. If $x = 1$, does $\frac{4}{0}$ . . . forget it. You can't divide by 0. Not ever. Period. Try (D). If $x = 2$, does $\frac{4}{1} = \frac{3}{2}$? No way. Try (E). If $x = 3$, $\frac{4}{2} = \frac{4}{2}$. Yes. Remember to avoid trying negatives [like choice (A)] unless they're

   all you have left or you have some reason to think they'll be right.

5. **E** Take the directions of the problem one at a time. The product of the digits = 6, so cross out (C). Now for step two. Subtract the tens digit from the units digit, and look for 5. (E) does it. If you picked (A), you subtracted the units digit from the tens digit, which means you don't know the definitions (see the definitions review at the beginning of the Arithmetic section) or—even more horrible—you didn't reread the question to see what your next direction was. Always reread the question before continuing on to the next step. We are human, after all.

6. **D** Try (C) first. Does 400 • 49 = 16,000? No, and hopefully you just estimate that and don't bother doing it, with or without your calculator. How about (D)? 400(40) = 16,000. Yep. If you picked (A), you miscounted the zeros. Try checking your answers on your calculator.

7. **C** Fabulous plugging in question. Try (C) first. Let's convert 0.5 to a

   fraction, because we like fractions better than decimals and because

   the question has a fraction in it. If the radius is $\frac{1}{2}$, the area is

   $\pi\left(\frac{1}{2}\right)^2 = \pi\left(\frac{1}{4}\right) = \frac{\pi}{4}$. Stick a fork in us, we're done.

HARD

8. **B** Try (D) first because the question is about percents and 100 is easy to do. 20% of 100 is 20. 100% of 100 − 70 is 30. Does 30 − 20 = 46? Nah. Try (B). 20% of 120 is 24. 120% of 50 is 60. Does 60 − 24 = 36? Yes.

9. **D** Try (C) first. If $y = 8$, then $x^2 = 8^3$. $8^3 = 512$. If $x^2 = 512$, x isn't an integer. Forget (C). Try (D). If $y = 4$, then $x^2 = 4^3$. $x^2 = 64$; $x = 8$. Now try them in the second equation: $(8 − 4)^2 = 2(8)$. $4^2 = 16$. It works. Notice that when (C) didn't work, we went with a smaller number because it was easier.

10. **B** First, write in 2π beside arc DB. Now try (C). If the area is 16π, the radius is 4. Write in 4 beside the two radii, and also DB, because $OD = DB$. Aha! That makes triangle DOB equilateral! Since angle DOB is $60°$, and $\frac{60}{360} = \frac{1}{6}$, that makes arc DB $\frac{1}{6}$ of the circumference. Remember our radius is 4, so the circumference is 8π. Uh oh— 2π is not $\frac{1}{6}$ of 8π. So cross off (C). But at least now we know what to do. Try (B). If the area is 36π, the radius is 6 and the circumference is 12π. $\frac{1}{6}$ of 12π is 2π. Yeah! Did that seem really painful? It was a lot of work, but then, it was a hard question. The reason plugging in is a good technique for this problem is that if you plug in the answer choices, you get to move through the question like a robot, one step after the other, and you don't have to depend on a flash of insight.

PROBLEM SET 5: ESTIMATING

EASY

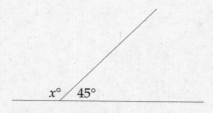

1. What is the value of 2x?

   (A) 360
   (B) 270
   (C) 135
   (D) 90
   (E) 67.5

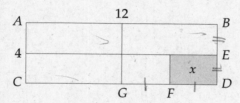

2. If F is equidistant from G and D, and E is equidistant from B and D, what fractional part of rectangle ABDC is area x?

   (A) $\frac{1}{16}$

   (B) $\frac{1}{8}$

   (C) $\frac{1}{4}$

   (D) $\frac{1}{3}$

   (E) $\frac{1}{2}$

3. If Sarah bought 12 pies for $30, how many pies could she have bought for $37.50 at the same rate?

(A) 9
(B) 10
(C) 12
(D) 14
(E) 15

$$\frac{12}{30} = \frac{x}{37.5}$$

MEDIUM

4. If a runner completes one lap of a track in 64 seconds, approximately how many minutes will it take her to run 40 laps at the same speed?

(A) 25
(B) 30
(C) 43
(D) 52
(E) 128

$$\frac{1}{64} = \frac{40}{x}$$
$$= x$$

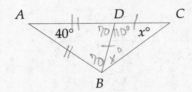

5. In the figure above, $BD = DC$ and $AB = AD$. What is the value of x?

(A) 110
(B) 70
(C) 55
(D) 35
(E) 15

6. Martina wants to buy as many felt-tip pens as possible for $10. If the pens cost between $1.75 and $2.30, what is the greatest number of pens Martina can buy?

(A) 4
(B) 5
(C) 6
(D) 7
(E) 8

7. 1.2 is what percent of 600?

(A) 0.002%
(B) 0.2%
(C) 5%
(D) 20%
(E) 500%

$$\frac{1.2}{600} \times 100$$

HARD

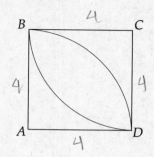

8. In the figure above, *ABCD* is a square with sides of 4. What is the length of arc *BD*?

(A) 8π
(B) 4π
(C) 3π
(D) 2π
(E) π

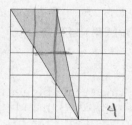

9. Each of the small squares in the figure above has an area of 4. If the shortest side of the triangle is equal in length to 2 sides of a small square, what is the area of the shaded triangle?

(A) 160
(B) 40
(C) 24
(D) 20
(E) 16

S = 2

$\frac{1}{2}$ 4 10

2 · 10 = 20

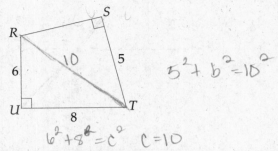

Note: Figure not drawn to scale.

10. In the figure above, what is the length of RS?

(A) 10

(B) $5\sqrt{3}$

(C) 8

(D) $\sqrt{5}$

(E) $2\sqrt{3}$

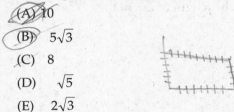

Answers and Explanations: Problem Set 5

Easy

1. **B** Estimate first: x looks pretty big, doesn't it? Bigger than 90? Yes. So $2x$ will be bigger than 180. Cross out (C), (D), and (E). Now figure out exactly what x is. $x + 45 = 180$, so x is 135. $2x = 270$.

2. **B** Use your eyeballs and compare against the answer choices. Does x look like $\frac{1}{2}$ of the rectangle? No? Cross out (E). What about $\frac{1}{3}$? Cross out (D). $\frac{1}{4}$? Cross out (C). Could you fit 16 xs in the rectangle? No—cross out (A). It's also helpful to draw more boxes in the figure, and then you could count them up:

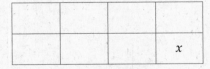

3. **E** $37.50 is going to buy more pies than $30, right? So cross out anything less than or equal to 12. Say goodbye to (A), (B), and (C). Now use your calculator and divide 30 by 12. You get 2.50—that's the cost per pie. Divide 37.5 by 2.50 and you get 15, which is the number of pies Sarah can buy for $37.50. You could also set up a proportion if you want:

$$\frac{pies}{\$} : \frac{12}{30} = \frac{x}{37.50}$$

MEDIUM

4. **C** The runner takes a little over a minute to run one lap, so it will take her a little more than 40 minutes to run 40 laps. The proportion would be:

$$\frac{1}{64} = \frac{40}{x}$$

So $x = 2{,}560$. Now convert the seconds to minutes by dividing 2,560 by 60. You get 42.666. Isn't estimating a lot faster?

5. **D** First just eyeball the angle. It's smaller than 90°. It's close to angle *BAD*, which is marked 40. You're down to (C) and (D). Is it a little smaller than *BAD* or 15° bigger than *BAD*? Go for it! You can always come back and check your answer the long way if you have time.

The long way: *BAD* is isosceles, since $AB = AD$. The two base angles of $BAD = 140$, so each is 70°. If $\angle BDA = 70°$, then $\angle BDC$ is 110°. Triangle *BDC* is isosceles too, with $\angle DCB$ and $\angle CBD = x°$. $2x = 70$, so $x = 35°$. Now admit it—isn't estimating easier?

6. **B** If Martina wants to buy as many pens as possible, she wants to buy the cheapest ones she can. Try plugging in the answer choices. Let's start with (C). If she buys 6 for $1.75, that equals $10.50. A bit more than $10, so pick the next lowest answer choice.

7. **B** 600 is pretty big, and 1.2 is pretty tiny. So you should be looking for a pretty small percentage. Cross out (D) and (E), and maybe even (C). Then use your calculator. The easiest way to figure out your next step would be to set up a proportion:

$$\frac{1.2}{600} = \frac{x}{100}$$

Or transform the sentence:

$$1.2 = \frac{x}{100} \cdot 600$$

Only 0.2, (B), fits the proportion.

Hard

8. **D** First mark the sides of the square with 4. Now estimate the length of *BD*, based on the side of the square. Think of the side of the square as a piece of spaghetti that you are going to drape over *BD*. So *BD* is longer than 4. Maybe around 6? Now go to the answers, and substitute 3 for π. (We know, π = 3.14, but you don't have to be so exact. We're just estimating.) Choice (A) is around 24. Way too big. (B) is around 12, (C) is around 9, and (D) is around 6. E is too small. We'd pick (D) and move on.

9. **D** When you estimate, remember that each shaded square has an area of 4. It's tricky to do this exactly, because mostly only slivers of squares are shaded. So fake it. Almost 2 full squares at the top, another square on the next row (that's 3 so far) and then slivers on the next 3 rows that make up about 2 full squares. So we've got 5 squares each with area 4; the area of the triangle is around 20. Hey, let's pick (D) and take a nap.

Okay, okay, so you want to cross out (A) and (B) and then get the answer exactly? We can do that. If each square has an area of 4, then the side of a little square is 2. Write that on the figure, in a couple of places. Now use the top of the triangle as the base. It equals 4. The other thing we need is the height, or altitude, of the triangle—and in this case, the height is equal to a side of the big square, or 10. Using the formula for the area of a triangle (we know you didn't have to look that up—we just know it), plug 4 in for the base and 10 in for the height and you get 20 for the area.

10. **B** Hey, wake up! You can't estimate anything if the figure isn't drawn to scale! But you may want to re-draw the figure to make it look more like it's supposed to look. Now for the solution: Draw a line from *R* to *T*, slicing the figure into 2 triangles. Now all you have to do is use the Pythagorean theorem to calculate the lengths. Triangle *RUT* is a 6:8:10 triangle, a Pythagorean triple. Now for *RST*: $a^2 + 5^2 = 10^2$. So $a^2 = 75$ and $a = 5\sqrt{3}$.

PROBLEM SET 6: FACTORS, MULTIPLES, AND PRIMES

EASY

1. If t is even, which of the following expressions must be odd?

   (A) $t - 2$ 2 $t = 4$
   (B) t^2 16
   (C) $2(t + 1)$ 10
   (D) $t(t + 1)$ 20
   (E) $t + 3$ 7

2. If m is a multiple of 5, and n is a factor of 3, which of the following could equal 13?

   (A) mn 30
   (B) $m + n$ 13 $m = 10$
   (C) $\dfrac{m}{n}$ 10/3 $n = 3$
   (D) $\dfrac{n}{m}$ 3/10
   (E) $m - n$ 7

   Set A: $\{0, 1, 2, 3, 4, 5\}$
   Set B: $\{1, 2, 7, 9, 10\}$

3. How many members of Set A are factors of any member of Set B?   1 2 3 5

   (A) 2
   (B) 3
   (C) 4
   (D) 5
   (E) 6

MEDIUM

4. Which of the following equations is equal to $6y + 6x = 66$?

   (A) $33 = x + y$
   (B) $33 = 2y + 2x$ $y + x = 11$
   (C) $11 - x = y$
   (D) $11 - 2x = y$ $y = 11 - x$
   (E) $4y - 4x = 44$

5. If the greatest prime factor of 32 is *a*, and the least prime factor of 77 is *b*, then *ab* is divisible by which of the following numbers?

    (A) 3
    (B) 4
    (C) 8
    (D) 11
    (E) 14

    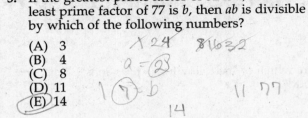

6. [*x*] is defined as the greatest prime factor of *x* minus the least prime factor of *x*. What is the value of $\dfrac{[20]}{[10]}$?

    (A) 10

    (B) 5

    (C) 2

    (D) 1

    (E) $\dfrac{1}{2}$

    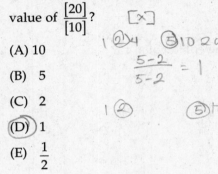

7. If *p* is the number of prime numbers between 65 and 75, then *p* =

    (A) 0
    (B) 1
    (C) 2
    (D) 3
    (E) 4

HARD

8. If r, s, and t are positive integers, and
   $rs = t$, then which of the following must be true?

   I. $r < t$
   II. $r \leq t$
   III. $s \geq t$

   (A) I only
   (B) II only
   (C) III only
   (D) I and III only
   (E) II and III only

(handwritten: $r=3$, $s=2$, $(3)(2)=6$, $t=6$; $r=5$, $s=1$, $t=5$)

9. If $12y = x^3$, and x and y are positive integers,
   what is the least possible value for y?

   (A) 3
   (B) 9
   (C) 18
   (D) 27
   (E) 64

(handwritten: $12(3)=x^3$; $12y=x^3$, $x=1$, $12y=1$, $y=1/12$)

10. The alarm of Clock A rings every 4 minutes, the
    alarm of Clock B rings every 6 minutes, and
    the alarm of Clock C rings every 7 minutes. If
    the alarms of all three clocks ring at 12:00 noon,
    the next time at which all the alarms will ring at
    exactly the same time is

    (A) 12:28 P.M.
    (B) 12:56 P.M.
    (C) 1:24 P.M.
    (D) 1:36 P.M.
    (E) 2:48 P.M.

(handwritten: 12; A 4; B 6; C 7)

(handwritten lists:
4 8 12 16 20 24 28 32 36 40 44 48
6 12 18 24 30 36 42 48 54 60 66 72
7 14 21 28 35 42
84 a✓ b✓ c✓)

Answers and Explanations: Problem Set 6

Easy

1. **E** Plug in an even number for t. How about $t = 2$? Now go to the answers, looking for something to be odd. (A) 0, (B) 4, (C) 6, (D) 10, and (E) 5. And remember that anything multiplied by an even number will be even, so you can eliminate (B), (C), and (D).

2. **B** Plug in again. Let's make $m = 10$ and $n = 3$. Run those through the answer choices, looking for 13. Choice (B) is $m + n$, or $10 + 3$ or 13. If you picked other numbers and didn't get an answer, don't get frustrated or think you're doing something wrong. Just pick another set of numbers, and make sure your numbers fit the directions of the problem (i.e., the number you pick for m has to be a multiple of 5, and the number you pick for n has to be either 1 or 3).

3. **C** Let's be methodical about this. Take each number in Set A, one at a time, and see if it divides evenly into anything in Set B. 0 isn't a factor of anything but 0. 1 is a factor of everything in Set B. Put a check by 1. 2 is a factor of 2, so put a check by 2. 3 is a factor of 9, so put a check by 3. 4 isn't a factor of anything in Set B. 5 is a factor of 10, so put a check by 5. How many checks do we have? Four of 'em.

Medium

4. **C** Try reducing the equation in the question first, by dividing the whole thing by 6. That leaves you with $x + y = 11$. That's the same as (C), if you just move the x to the other side.

5. **E** There's only one prime factor of 32, and it's 2. The prime factors of 77 are 7 and 11, so the smallest is 7. That makes $ab = 14$, which is certainly divisible by 14.

6. **D** This is a function question, as we're sure you noticed. First deal with [20]. The greatest prime factor of 20 is 5, and the least prime factor is 2. $5 - 2 = 3$, so [20] = 3. Now for [10]. The greatest prime factor of 10 is 5, and the least prime factor is 2. So [10] = $5 - 2 = 3$. $\frac{3}{3} = 1$.

7. **D** First write out the numbers: 66, 67, 68, 69, 70, 71, 72, 73, 74. Be methodical—cross out anything that's even: 66, 68, 70, 72, 74. Now cross out anything left that's divisible by 3: 69. Any number divisible by 4, 6, or 8 is even, and we've already crossed those out. Any number divisible by 9 is also divisible by 3, and we've crossed that out. All we have left is 7—we're left with 67, 71, and 73. None of them is divisible by 7, so they're all prime.

HARD

8. **B** Plug in. Let's make a little chart:

r	s	t
1	2	2
1	1	1
2	3	6

That should do it. Now check our numbers against I, II, and III. I isn't true if r, s, and t all equal 1. III isn't true if $r = 2$, $s = 3$, and $t = 6$. That leaves us with II.

Why bother with a chart? On *must be* questions, picking one set of numbers probably isn't going to be enough. This question is pretty tricky for a medium, because I is true except when all the variables equal 1. But then I and II only isn't a choice, so you have to disprove one of them.

9. **C** Solve this problem with a combination of factoring and plugging in. The question looks like this: $2 \times 2 \times 3y = x^3$. Now factor the answer choices. Choice (A) is $3 \cdot 1$. If you plug that in for y, does it give you a cube? Nope. (B) is $3 \cdot 3$. No good either. (C) is $2 \times 3 \times 3$—now we have $(2 \times 3)(2 \times 3)(2 \times 3) = x^3$. It works.

Another way to do this problem is more straightforward plugging in: Plug in the answers for y, and use your calculator to see if that product is a cube root. If your calculator doesn't have the x^y function, then make a list of cubes to see if the product is on it.

10. **C** Ouch—this one is ugly. You can't simply multiply $4 \times 6 \times 7$ and add 168 minutes to 12:00. You'll get (E), and while it's true that all 3 alarms would ring at 2:48, that's not the *earliest* time they would ring at the same time. (And that solution is too easy for a hard question.) Instead, factor the ringing rates, so you get (2×2), (2×3), and (7). The lowest common multiple will be $2 \times 2 \times 3 \times 7$. Four goes in evenly, and so do 6 and 7. Now multiply it, and you get 84, which is 1 hour and 24 minutes. Add that to 12:00, and you're done.

> **TIP:**
> When you're plugging in the answer choices, remember that if the question asks for the *least possible value*, start with the smallest answer choice. For *greatest possible value*, start with the biggest answer choice. That way you won't get caught picking an answer that works, but isn't the *least* or *greatest* answer that works.

PROBLEM SET 7: FRACTIONS, DECIMALS, AND PERCENTS

EASY

1. A big-screen TV is on sale at 15% off the regular price. If the regular price of the TV is $420, what is the sale price?

    (A) $63
    (B) $126
    (C) $357
    (D) $405
    (E) $435

2. Which of the following is the decimal form of
$$70 + \frac{7}{10} + \frac{3}{1000}?$$

    (A) 70.0703
    (B) 70.7003
    (C) 70.703
    (D) 70.73
    (E) 77.003

3. Six more than two-thirds of twelve is

    (A) 10
    (B) 12
    (C) 14
    (D) 18
    (E) 22

$$6 + \frac{2}{3}12$$

MEDIUM

4. Walking at a constant rate, Stuart takes 24 minutes to walk to the nearest bus stop, and $\frac{1}{3}$ of that time to walk to the movie theater. It takes him half the time to walk to school than it does for him to walk to the movie theater. How many minutes does it take Stuart to walk to school?

(A) 36
(B) 24
(C) 16
(D) 8
(E) 4

Handwritten: t = 24m — bus stop ; 8 m — movies ; 4m — S

5. What is the value of x if $\frac{\frac{1}{2}}{x} = 4$?

(A) 8

(B) 2

(C) $\frac{1}{2}$

(D) $\frac{1}{4}$

(E) $\frac{1}{8}$

Handwritten: $\frac{1}{2} = 4x$; $\frac{\frac{1}{2}}{4} = x$

6. If $x\%$ of y is 10, then $y\%$ of x is

(A) 1
(B) 5
(C) 10
(D) 50
(E) 90

Handwritten: $\cdot xy = 10$; $(.1)(100) = 10$; $(1)10 =$; $y = 100$; $x = 10\%$

7. A certain drink is made by adding 4 parts water to 1 part drink mix. If the amount of water is doubled, and the amount of drink mix is quadrupled, what percent of the new mixture is drink mix?

(A) 30%

(B) $33\frac{1}{3}$%

(C) 50%

(D) $66\frac{2}{3}$%

(E) 80%

Handwritten: $4w + 1D = 5P$
Handwritten: $8w + 4D = 12P$

HARD

8. Set A consists of distinct fractions, each of which has a numerator of 1 and a denominator d such that $1 < d < 8$, where d is an integer. If Set B consists of the reciprocals of the fractions with odd denominators in Set A, then the product of Set A and Set $B =$

(A) $\frac{1}{96}$

(B) $\frac{1}{48}$

(C) $\frac{1}{24}$

(D) 1

(E) 8

Handwritten: A $\frac{1}{d}$ $1 < d < 8$ $\frac{1}{2}$ $\frac{1}{3}$ $\frac{1}{4}$ $\frac{1}{5}$ $\frac{1}{6}$ $\frac{1}{7}$
Handwritten: B $\frac{3}{1}$ $\frac{5}{1}$ $\frac{7}{1}$
Handwritten: $(\frac{1}{2}$

9. For all values x, if x is even, x^* is defined as $0.5x$; if x is odd, x^* is defined as $\frac{x}{3}$. What is the value of $\frac{(6a)^*}{9^*}$?

(A) $2a$
(B) $3a$
(C) a^*
(D) $(2a)^*$
(E) $(4a)^*$

Handwritten: $6a = x$ $x^* = .5(6a) = 3a$
Handwritten: $9 = x$ $x^* = \frac{9}{3} = 3$
Handwritten: $(2a)^* = .5 2a = a$

10. If a, b, and c are distinct positive integers, and 10% of abc is 5, then $a + b$ could equal

(A) 1
(B) 3
(C) 5
(D) 8
(E) 25

[handwritten: $a+$ / a b c / $1+2$ 25 / 4 / $a=1$ $b=5$ $c=10$ / $abc=50$]

Answers and Explanations: Problem Set 7

Easy

1. **C** The numbers are too awkward to plug in, so do it the old-fashioned way: 15% of $420 is $0.15 \times 420 = 63$. $420 - 63 = 357$. Use your calculator.

2. **C** Take the pieces one at a time and eliminate. The first piece is 70: eliminate (E). The second piece is $\frac{7}{10}$, or 0.7. Eliminate (A). The last piece is $\frac{3}{1000}$, or 0.003. Eliminate (B) and (D). If you want to do the conversions on your calculator, that's cool. But adding the fractions together and then converting to a decimal would be a massive waste of your precious time, calculator or no calculator.

3. **C** Translate the problem into math language: $6 + \frac{2}{3} \times 12 =?$. Then, don't forget PEMDAS: Multiply before you add. $6 + \frac{2}{3}(12) = 6 + 8 = 14$.

Medium

4. **E** Start working from the 24 minutes it takes poor Stuart to walk to the bus stop. (Won't anybody give the guy a ride?) If it takes $\frac{1}{3}$ of 24 to walk to the movies, that's 8 minutes. If it takes him half of that time to walk to school, $\frac{1}{2}$ of 8 is 4. This question requires close reading more than anything else.

5. **E** Plugging in the answer choices wouldn't be a bad idea here—you can

   eliminate (A) and (B) pretty quickly that way. (C) gives you $\dfrac{\frac{1}{2}}{\frac{1}{1}} = 1$.

   (D) is $\dfrac{\frac{1}{2}}{\frac{1}{4}} = 2.$ E is $\dfrac{\frac{1}{2}}{\frac{1}{8}} = 4.$

6. **C** Let's plug in 20 for y, which makes $x = 50$. Plug those numbers into the second part: 20% of 50 = 10.

7. **B** First make a little chart: If you double the water and quadruple the mix, you get

water		mix
4	:	1
8	:	4

   Reread the question. It asks for the percentage of the new mixture that's

   drink mix. We've got $\dfrac{4\,(\text{mix})}{12\,(\text{total})}$, which equals $\dfrac{1}{3}$, or $33\dfrac{1}{3}\%$.

   If you made it almost to the end but picked (C), don't forget that you

   have to express the mix as a percentage of the total, not a percentage of

   the water.

Hard

8. **B** Whew. You have to read this carefully. Set A has different fractions, each

   with a numerator of 1. (You might as well write them down like that

   and fill in the denominators when you get there.) The denominators are

   between 1 and 8. That gives you Set A: $\dfrac{1}{2}, \dfrac{1}{3}, \dfrac{1}{4}, \dfrac{1}{5}, \dfrac{1}{6}, \dfrac{1}{7}$. Set B has the

   reciprocals of the members of Set A with odd denominators, so Set B:

   $\dfrac{3}{1}, \dfrac{5}{1}, \dfrac{7}{1}$. Now we're going to multiply the sets together—see how the

   fractions that have reciprocals cancel each other out? You're left with

   $\dfrac{1}{2} \times \dfrac{1}{4} \times \dfrac{1}{6}$, which is $\dfrac{1}{48}$.

9. **D** It's a function, so just follow the directions. Looking at the numerator, $6a$ has to be even because it has an even number as a factor. (Or plug in any low number for a.) Since $6a$ is even, follow the first direction: $6a \times 0.5 = 3a$. Now for the denominator: 9 is odd, so follow the second direction. $\frac{9}{3} = 3$. So $\frac{(6a)^*}{9^*} = \frac{3a}{3} = a$. Did you pick (C)? Well, sorry, we aren't getting off that easy. (C), (D), and (E) are functions, too, so we have to translate them, looking for our answer, a. Skip (A) and (B). For (D), $(2a)$ is even, so $(2a)^* = 2a \times 0.5 = a$. *Finito.*

10. **B** First translate the middle part of the problem into an equation. 10% of abc is 5 translates to $\frac{10}{100} \cdot abc = 5$. Now solve for abc, and you get $abc = 50$. Reread the question. Each variable is different, each is positive, and multiplied together they produce 50. Now plug in the answer choices, and remember that the answers represent $a + b$. Choice (A) is silly, because it would make a and b fractions, and they can't be fractions. In (B), $a + b$ would have to be $1 + 2$. If $a = 1$ and $b = 2$ and $abc = 50$, what is c? $c = 25$, so it works.

TIP:

A couple of reminders: If you are making mistakes on the easy and medium problems, don't spend a lot of time—if any—working on the hard problems. You need to hone your skills first; you may want to go back to the review section and do some work before continuing. And don't forget, you probably want to leave some questions blank on the real thing.

Speaking of leaving questions blank, question 9 would be a fine choice to avoid entirely. Long functions in the hard problems can be really nasty.

PROBLEM SET 8: RATIOS, PROPORTIONS, AND PROBABILITIES

Easy

1. If $\dfrac{8}{x} = \dfrac{2}{3}$, then $x =$

   (A) 12
   (B) 10
   (C) 6
   (D) 4
   (E) 3

   $24 = 2x$

   $x = 12$

2. A factory produces 6,000 plates per day. If one out of 15 plates is broken, how many unbroken plates does the factory produce each day?

   (A) 5800
   (B) 5600
   (C) 1500
   (D) 800
   (E) 400

   $6000 \, p/o$

   $\dfrac{1}{15} = br$

   $\dfrac{14}{15} = \dfrac{x}{6000}$

   $84000 = 15x$

3. It takes 4 friends 24 minutes to wash all the windows in Maria's house. The friends all work at the same rate. How long would it take 8 friends, working at the same rate, to wash all the windows in Maria's house?

   (A) 96
   (B) 32
   (C) 20
   (D) 12
   (E) 8

   $\dfrac{4f}{24m} \qquad \dfrac{8f}{x} \qquad \dfrac{24}{x} = \dfrac{4}{8}$

   $192 \qquad 4x$

Medium

4. In a certain classroom, there is an equal number of boys and girls. If 2 girls and 1 boy left to go home, the ratio of boys to girls in the room would be 4:3. How many girls are in the classroom now before anyone leaves?

   (A) 2
   (B) 3
   (C) 4
   (D) 5
   (E) 6

   $b = g$

   $-2g \quad -1b$

   $5 = 5$

   $b = g$

   $-1 \quad 2$

   $\overline{}$

   $4 \quad 3$

5. The value of t is inversely proportional to the value of w. If value of w increases by a factor of 5, what happens to the value of t?

(A) t increases by a factor of 5.
(B) t increases by a factor of 2.
(C) t remains constant.
(D) t decreases by a factor of 2.
(E) t decreases by a factor of 5.

6. A drawer holds only blue socks and white socks. If the ratio of blue socks to white socks is 4:3, which of the following could be the total number of socks in the drawer?

(A) 4
(B) 7
(C) 8
(D) 12
(E) 24

7. The probability of choosing a caramel from a certain bag of candy is $\frac{1}{5}$, and the probability of choosing a butterscotch is $\frac{5}{8}$. If the bag contains 40 pieces of candy, and the only types of candy in the bag are caramel, butterscotch, and fudge, how many pieces of fudge are in the bag?

(A) 5
(B) 7
(C) 8
(D) 16
(E) 25

HARD

8. The ratio of $\frac{1}{6} : \frac{1}{5}$ is equal to the ratio of 35 to

(A) 24
(B) 30
(C) 36
(D) 42
(E) 45

9. An artist makes a certain shade of green paint by mixing blue and yellow in a ratio of 3:4. She makes orange by mixing red and yellow in a ratio of 2:3. If on one day she mixes both green and orange and uses equal amounts of blue and red paint, what fractional part of the paint that she uses is yellow?

(A) $\dfrac{7}{12}$

(B) $\dfrac{17}{29}$

(C) $\dfrac{7}{5}$

(D) $\dfrac{17}{12}$

(E) $\dfrac{9}{6}$

10. The areas of two circles are in a ratio of 4:9. If both radii are integers, and $r_1 - r_2 = 2$, which of the following is the radius of the larger circle?

(A) 4
(B) 5
(C) 6
(D) 8
(E) 9

ANSWERS AND EXPLANATIONS: PROBLEM SET 8

EASY

1. **A** Cross-multiply and you get $24 = 2x$, so $x = 12$.

2. **B** First estimate. You're looking for the number of unbroken plates—if only one broke out of 15, there should be a lot of unbroken plates, right? Cross out (C), (D), and (E). Now set up a proportion:

$$\frac{\text{broken}}{\text{total}} = \frac{1}{15} = \frac{x}{6000}$$

And cross-multiply. You get $6000 = 15x$, so using your calculator, $x = 400$. That's the number of broken plates, so subtract 400 from 6000 and you've got the answer. If you picked (E), you could have gotten the problem right if you had either estimated first or reread the question right before you answered it.

3. **D** There are twice as many people, so the work will go twice as fast. You can't set up a normal proportion because it's an inverse proportion—the more people you have, the less time the work takes. So if you multiply the number of people by 2, you divide the work time by 2. Don't forget to use your common sense.

MEDIUM

4. **D** Let's plug in the answer choices, shall we? Try (C) first. If there are 4 girls, there are 4 boys, since the numbers start out equal. Now subtract 1 boy and 2 girls and you get 3:2. No good. Try (D) 5 boys, 5 girls, 1 boy and 2 girls leave—that gives us 4:3. That's why we love plugging in.

5. **E** Since no values were given, try plugging in values of your own to test what happens. If t starts out as 10 and w starts out as 5, we can set up the formula for inverse variation as follows: $t_1 w_1 = t_2 w_2$. In this case, the t_1 is 10, w_1 is 5, and w_2 is 25 (since we multiply it by 5). So set up the equation as: $10 \times 5 = t_2 \times 25$. $\frac{50}{25} t = 2$. So what happened to the value of t? It decreased by a factor of 5.

6. **B** The total must be the sum of the numbers in a ratio, or a multiple of that sum. In this case, $4 + 3 = 7$, so the number of socks could be 7 or any multiple of 7. (You can have fractions in a ratio, it's true, but not when you're dealing with socks or people or anything that you can't chop into pieces. And probably not on a medium question, either.)

7. **B** Here's what to do: Take $\frac{1}{5}$ of 40, which is 8 caramels. Take $\frac{5}{8}$ of 40, which is 25 butterscotches. The caramels and the butterscotches are $8 + 25 = 33$. Subtract that from 40 and you've got the fudge.

HARD

8. **D** First multiply the ratio by something big to get rid of the fraction. Any multiple of 6 and 5 will do. So $30\left(\frac{1}{6}\right):30\left(\frac{1}{5}\right) = 5:6$. Now we've got $5:6 = 35:x$. Since 35 is 5×7, x is 6×7, or 42. The new ratio is 35:42, which is the same as 5:6.

9. **B** Write down your ratios and label them neatly. You have

$$\frac{b{:}y}{3{:}4} \qquad \frac{r{:}y}{2{:}3}$$

If the artist uses equal amounts of blue and red, we have to multiply each ratio:

$$\frac{b:y}{(2)(3:4)} \qquad \frac{r:y}{(2:3)(3)}$$

The result is

$$\frac{b{:}y}{6{:}8} \qquad \frac{r{:}y}{6{:}9}$$

The yellow is 8 parts + 9 parts = 17 parts, and the total is 6 + 8 + 6 + 9 = 29 parts. On complicated ratio problems, it's important, to organize the information legibly and label everything as you go along, or else you'll find yourself looking at a bunch of meaningless numbers.

10. **C** Plug in the answer choices! Start with (C) If the larger radius is 6, the smaller radius is 2 less than that, or 4. The area of the smaller circle = 16π, and the area of the larger circle is 36π. $16\pi{:}36\pi$ is a ratio of 4:9. (Just divide the whole ratio by 4) If you picked (E), you must've had a momentary blackout—that answer is way too appealing to be right on a hard question. If you're going to guess, guess something less obvious.

PROBLEM SET 9: AVERAGES

EASY

1. Three consecutive integers add up to 258. What is the smallest integer?

   (A) 58
   (B) 85
   (C) 86
   (D) 89
   (E) 94

2. If the average (arithmetic mean) of x, $2x$, and 15 is 9, then $x =$

   (A) 2
   (B) 4
   (C) 7
   (D) 8
   (E) 9

   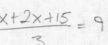

   $$\frac{x+2x+15}{3} = 9$$

   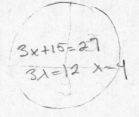

   $3x + 15 = 27$
   $3x = 12 \quad x = 4$

a	1, 2, 3, 4, 5 ~~3~~	15
b	21, 22, 23, 24, 25	~~H~~ 115

3. What is the mean of the sum of the members of a + the sum of the numbers of b?

   (A) 13
   (B) 18
   (C) 21
   (D) 25
   (E) 26

MEDIUM

4. The average (arithmetic mean) of 4 numbers is 36. If the two middle numbers add up to 62, what is the average of the smallest and largest numbers?

   (A) 20
   (B) 36
   (C) 41
   (D) 72
   (E) 82

   $$\frac{A+B+C+D}{4} = 36$$

   $$\frac{A+62+D}{4} = 36$$

   $A + 62 + D = 144$

   $A + D = 82$

Questions 5–6 refer to the following definition.

For all numbers x and y, $(x, y)!$ is defined as the average of x and y.

5. $(2, 10)! - (2, 2)! =$

    (A) $(2, 5)!$
    (B) $(2, 10)!$
    (C) $(3, 6)!$
    (D) $(5, 4)!$
    (E) $(7, 1)!$

6. Which of the following represents $(a, b, c)!$?

    (A) $3abc$

    (B) abc

    (C) $\dfrac{abc}{2}$

    (D) $\dfrac{a+b+c}{3}$

    (E) $\dfrac{3}{a+b+c}$

7. Dixie spent an average of x dollars on each of 5 shirts and an average of y dollars on each of 3 hats. In terms of x and y, how many dollars did she spend on shirts and hats?

    (A) $5x + 3y$
    (B) $3x + 5y$
    (C) $15(x + y)$
    (D) $8xy$
    (E) $15xy$

HARD

8. Fred played a total of 7 rounds of golf, and the 7 scores he received were consecutive integers. If Fred's lowest score was g, then in terms of g, what was his average score for all 7 rounds?

    (A) $\dfrac{g+7}{7}$

    (B) $\dfrac{7(g+1)}{g}$

    (C) $7g + 7$

    (D) $g + 3$

    (E) $g + 7$

9. A certain car can travel on a highway for 300 miles on 12 gallons of gas and in a city for 270 miles on 15 gallons of gas. If the car uses an equal number of gallons for highway driving and city driving, what is the car's average number of miles per gallon?

(A) 15
(B) 18.5
(C) 20
(D) 21.5
(E) 25

[handwritten: highway $\frac{300m}{12\,g}$ city $\frac{270m}{15\,g}$]

[handwritten: $\frac{300+270}{12+15} = \frac{570}{27}$]

10. On 5 math tests, Gloria had an average score of 86. If all test scores are integers, what is the lowest average score Gloria can receive on the remaining 3 tests if she wants to finish the semester with an average score of 90 or higher?

(A) 90
(B) 92
(C) 94
(D) 96
(E) 97

[handwritten: $\frac{A+B+C+D+E}{5} = 86$]

[handwritten: $\frac{430+F+G+H}{8} = 90$]

[handwritten: $F+G+H = 290$]

ANSWERS AND EXPLANATIONS: PROBLEM SET 9

EASY

1. **B** If the three integers add up to 258, then their average is 258 ÷ 3, or 86. Since the integers are consecutive, they must be 85, 86, and 87. Check it on your calculator. If you picked (C), what did you do wrong? Forget what the question asked for? Divide 258 by 3 and then quit? Even easy problems may have more than one step. This would also be a good question to plug in the answer choices.

2. **B** Plug in the answer choices. Try (C) first: If $x = 7$, is the average of 14, 7, and 15 equal to 9? Doesn't that average look too big? Try (B). Is the average of 4, 8, and 15 equal to 9? You bet.

3. **A** Time for an adding trick: First add up a and get 15. For b, add the tens digits and the units digits separately: $5 \times 20 = 100$, and you already know that $1 + 2 + 3 + 4 + 5 = 15$, because you just added it. So $b = 100 + 15 = 115$. Now add a and b to get 130, and divide by the number of numbers in both sets, which is 10. And of course, you should use your calculator. When you have a lot of numbers to punch in, be sure to look at each one as it appears in the window so that if you punch in 10 instead of 100, you catch it. Estimating will help, too.

MEDIUM

4. **C** If the average of the numbers is 36, then their sum is $4 \times 36 = 144$. If the 2 middle numbers equal 62, subtract them from the sum, and $144 - 62 = 82$. 82 is the sum of the remaining numbers, so to get their average, divide by 2.

5. **E** All we have to do is take the average of the 2 numbers in the parentheses. (2, 10)! is the average of 2 and 10, which is 6. (2, 2)! is the average of 2 and 2, which is 2. $6 - 2 = 4$. Circle 4. Now we have to translate the answer choices, since they are functions as well. (E) is the average of 7 and 1, which is 4.

6. **D** To take the average of a set of numbers, add them up and divide by the number in the set. So all we have to do is add a, b, and c and divide by 3.

7. **A** Plug in. Let $x = 2$. If Dixie spent an average of $2 a shirt, then she spent a total of $10 on shirts. Let $y = 4$, and she spent an average of $4 a hat, for a total of $12. Our total is $10 + 12 = \$22$. Circle that. Now on to the answer choices, and $x = 2$ and $y = 4$. (A) is $5(2) + 3(4) = 22$. Bingo.

HARD

8. **D** Plug in. Let's say Fred scored a 2 on his first round, so $g = 2$. (We know that's an impossible golf score, but who cares? We want a low number to work with.) If his scores were consecutive numbers, his scores would be 2, 3, 4, 5, 6, 7, 8. The average of those is 5. Circle 5. Plug in 2 for g in the answers and you get (D): $2 + 3 = 5$.

9. **D** Figure the highway first. 300 miles on 12 gallons is $300 \div 12 = 25$ miles per gallon. In the city, $270 \div 15 = 18$ miles per gallon. Since the car uses an equal number of gallons on the highway and in the city, we can average the miles per gallon for each, and the average of 25 and 18 is 21.5.

10. **E** If Gloria averaged 86 on 5 tests, her total number of points so far is $86 \times 5 = 430$. If she wants to get an average of 90 on 8 tests, she needs a grand total of $90 \times 8 = 720$ points. So dear Gloria has 3 tests to make up the difference of 720 and 430, which is 290. If you divide 290 by 3, you get 96.66—so she needs to get an average of 97 on the remaining 3 tests.

PROBLEM SET 10:
STANDARD DEVIATION, INTERSECTION, AND UNION

EASY

1. Set S is made up of all of the multiples of 6, and set T is made up of all of the multiples of 9. If set U is the union of sets S and T, which of the following is true of set U?

   (A) Set U contains only even values.
   (B) Set U contains only odd values.
   (C) Set U contains only multiples of 3.
   (D) Set U contains only multiples of 6.
   (E) Set U contains only multiples of 9.

2. Set C is composed of all of the factors of 60, and set D is composed of all of the factors of 80. Which of the following correctly gives the set that is the result of $C \cap D$?

   (A) {1, 2, 5, 10}
   (B) {1, 2, 4, 5, 10, 20}
   (C) {1, 2, 4, 5, 10, 15, 20}
   (D) {2, 3, 4, 5, 10, 15, 16, 20}
   (E) {1, 2, 3, 4, 5, 6, 8, 10, 12, 15, 16, 20}

{1, 3, 5, 15}

3. The set shown above can be defined by which of the following?

> I. {factors of 15}
> II. {factors of 15} ∩ {factors of 30}
> III. {factors of 30} ∩ {factors of 60}

(A) I only
(B) II only
(C) I and II only
(D) I and III only
(E) I, II, and III

MEDIUM

4. Set A consists of 7 terms with a mode of 9, and set B consists of 10 terms with a mode of 11. What is largest number of terms that can be found in the set created by $A \cap B$?

(A) 3
(B) 4
(C) 5
(D) 6
(E) 7

5. The average rainfall in Cairo is 24.8 mm per year. If the standard deviation for the rainfall is 2.7 mm, which of the following amounts of rain is within 1 standard deviation of the average?

(A) 21.7 mm
(B) 22.1 mm
(C) 22.3 mm
(D) 27.5 mm
(E) 29.1 mm

$$M: \{1, 3, 5, 7, 10, 16\}$$
$$N: \{7, 12, 15, 16, 22, 24\}$$
$$O: \{7, 16\}$$

6. Sets M, N, and O are shown above. Which of the following also correctly identifies the values of set O?

> I. $M \cup N$
> II. $M \cap N$
> III. Mean of set M and mean of set N

(A) III only
(B) I and II only
(C) II and III only
(D) I and III only
(E) None

$$P: \{1, 16, 27, 40\}$$
$$Q: \{12, 19, 22, 27\}$$
$$R: \{9, 11, 17, 32\}$$

7. Sets P, Q, and R are shown above. Which of the
    following has the greatest standard deviation?

    (A) Set P
    (B) Set Q
    (C) Set R
    (D) $P \cup Q$
    (E) $Q \cup R$

HARD

8. The average score on a test in Carlena's class
    is an 81% with a standard deviation of 7%. If
    Carlena gets a c% on the test, and she receives a
    score that is *not* within 2 standard deviations of
    the mean, which of the following correctly gives
    the range of scores that Carlena could <u>NOT</u>
    have received?

    (A) $67\% < c < 95\%$
    (B) $67\% < c < 81\%$
    (C) $c < 67\%$
    (D) $74\% < \text{test score} < 88\%$
    (E) $c < 67\%$ and $c > 95\%$

$$A: \{3, 6, 8, 9, 11, 15\}$$
$$B: \{1, 4, 6, 8, 13, 17, 22\}$$
$$C: \{2, 5, 6, 9, 17, 19\}$$

9. Sets A, B, and C are shown above. What is the
    set that is the result of $A \cup (B \cap C)$?

    (A) $\{3, 6, 6, 8, 9, 11, 15, 17\}$
    (B) $\{3, 6, 8, 9, 11, 15, 17\}$
    (C) $\{6\}$
    (D) $\{6, 17\}$
    (E) $\{1, 2, 3, 4, 11, 13, 15, 22\}$

10. Set F consists of all of the prime numbers from
    1 to 20 inclusive, and set G consists of all of the
    odd numbers from 1 to 20 inclusive. If f is the
    number of values in set F, g is the number of
    values in set G, and j is the number of values in
    $F \cup G$, which of the following gives the correct
    value of $f(j - g)$?

    (A) 4
    (B) 8
    (C) 10
    (D) 11
    (E) 18

Answers and Explanations: Problem Set 10

Easy

1. **C** Since set U is the union of the other two sets, it includes all of the values that are in each set. Therefore, it contains odd and even values, some of which are multiples of 6 and some of which are multiples of 9. One thing that all of the values are, however, are multiples of 3, so (C) is the best answer.

2. **B** The symbol $\cap$ means to look for the intersection of the two sets, which is the list of numbers that both sets have. List out both set D and set C to see what the combination should look like: $C = \{1, 2, 3, 4, 5, 6, 10, 12, 15, 20, 30, 60\}$, $D = \{1, 2, 4, 5, 8, 10, 16, 20, 40, 80\}$, so the values that are in both sets are: $\{1, 2, 4, 5, 10, 20\}$.

3. **C** The list shown is a list of the factors of 15, so I definitely works, which allows us to eliminate (B). Since 15 divides into 30, all of the factors of 15 will also be factors of 30, so the intersection of the factors of 15 and 30 will still just be the factors of 15. Since II also works, cross out (A) and (D). The intersection of the factors of 30 and 60 will actually just be the factors of 30, since all factors of 30 are also factors of 60. However, that is not what the list at the top represents, so III doesn't work: cross out (E).

Medium

4. **E** For set A to have a mode of 9, it has to at least have two terms that are 9. Since set B has more available terms, let's see if it is possible that all of the values of set A are contained within set B. If set B contains three terms that are 11, then the other seven terms of set B could be the seven terms from set A. This still allows 11 to be the mode of set B, since there are three 11s and only two 9s. The correct answer, therefore, is (E). Two possible sets for A and B are: $A = \{1, 2, 3, 4, 5, 9, 9\}$ and $B = \{1, 2, 3, 4, 5, 9, 9, 11, 11, 11\}$.

5. **C** If the average is 24.8 mm, and the standard deviation is 2.7 mm, then to fall within 1 standard deviation, the amount of rainfall must fall in between 22.1 mm and 27.5 mm. Only one value falls within that range: (C).

6. **C** The union of sets M and N would not result in set O, so cross out (B) and (D). The intersection of sets M and N would result in set O, so eliminate any answer that doesn't contain II, which eliminates (A) and (E), leaving only (C).

7. **A** The set with the largest range of values will have the largest standard deviation. Of the three, set P definitely has the largest range, so cross out (B) and (C). When doing the union of sets P and Q, the range doesn't change, but there are more values. This only decreases the standard deviation, since the values are clustered more around whatever the average is. Cross out (D) and also (E) because the union of sets Q and R has a smaller range and more values than set P.

HARD

8. **A** Since Carlena received a score that is *not* within 2 standard deviations, we need to figure out what scores are 2 standard deviations above and below the average. 1 standard deviation is 7%, so 2 standard deviations is 14%. So the scores that the range should be defined by are 67% and 95%. However, we are looking for a range of scores that Carlena *couldn't* have received, so (A) is the correct answer.

9. **B** First start with the sets inside the parenthesis. The problem asks us to find the intersection of sets B and C. There are only 2 numbers that are common to both sets: {6, 17}. Now take the newly created set and find the union of it with set A. This should include all of the values either of the sets have, minus any repeats. So the final set should include all of the numbers in set A, with 17 added in. However, it should not contain two 6s, so (B) is the best answer.

10. **B** Let's figure out what each set is first. Set F is {2, 3, 5, 7, 11, 13, 17, 19}, and set G is {1, 3, 5, 7, 9, 11, 13, 15, 17, 19}, which means that the union of the two sets is {1, 2, 3, 5, 7, 9, 11, 13, 15, 17, 19}. Now that you know the sets, find out how many terms are in each: $f = 8$, $g = 10$, and $j = 11$. So the value of $8 \times (11 - 10) = 8$, or (B).

PROBLEM SET 11: EXPONENTS AND ROOTS

EASY

1. If $t^3 = -8$, then $t^2 =$

   (A) −4
   (B) −2
   (C) 2
   (D) 4
   (E) 8

2. If $r + \sqrt{r} = s^2 - 6$ and $r = 25$, then $s =$

   (A) 5
   (B) 6
   (C) 7
   (D) 9
   (E) 19

   $25 + 5 = s^2 - 6$
   $24 = s^2$

3. If $3^x = 27$, then $4^x =$

   (A) 8
   (B) 12
   (C) 16
   (D) 64
   (E) 128

   $3^x = 27 \quad x = 3$
   $\dfrac{4}{64}$

MEDIUM

4. For all integers x and y, let

    $\bigstar (x + y) = \dfrac{x^2}{y^2}$. What is the value of

    $\bigstar (2 + y) \times \bigstar (y + 1)$?

    (A) 16
    (B) 9
    (C) 5
    (D) 4
    (E) 3

    $\dfrac{2^2}{y^2} \times \dfrac{y^2}{1^2} = \dfrac{4}{1}$

5. If p and k are integers, and $\sqrt{p} = 3^3 \sqrt{k}$, then p
    must be

    (A) odd
    (B) even
    (C) positive
    (D) negative
    (E) greater than 1

    $k = 4$

    $\sqrt{p} = 27 \cdot 2$

    $\sqrt{p} = 54 \qquad p = 54^2$

    $\dfrac{\overset{1}{27}}{2} \cdot \dfrac{}{54}$

6. $\dfrac{\sqrt{a} \cdot \sqrt{b}}{3\sqrt{a} - 2\sqrt{a}} =$

    $\dfrac{\sqrt{ab}}{\sqrt{a}} = \sqrt{b}$

    (A) $\quad \dfrac{\sqrt{b}}{\sqrt{a}}$

    (B) $\quad \sqrt{b}$

    (C) $\quad \dfrac{2\sqrt{a}}{b}$

    (D) $\quad \sqrt{ab}$

    (E) $\quad \sqrt{a^2 b}$

7. If $\dfrac{8^{\frac{2}{3}}}{x^2} = 20x^{-3}$, what is the value of x?

    (A) 5

    (B) $8^{\frac{2}{3}}$

    (C) $\dfrac{1}{20}$

    (D) 80

    (E) 160

    $\dfrac{8^{2/3}}{x^2} = \dfrac{20}{x^3}$

    $\dfrac{x^3}{x^2} = \dfrac{20}{8^{2/3}}$

    $x = \dfrac{20}{8^{2/3}}$

HARD

8. If $0 > a^3bc^6$, then which of the following must be true?

   I. *ab* is positive
   II. *ab* is negative
   III. *abc* is negative

   (A) I only
   (B) II only
   (C) III only
   (D) I and III only
   (E) II and III only

   [handwritten: a = 2, b = -1, c = 1, a =.]
   [handwritten: $a^3bc^6 = 8(-1)(1) = -8$]
   [handwritten: $0 > -8$]

9. For positive integers p, t, x, and y, if $p^x = t^y$

   and $x - y = 3$, which of the following CANNOT

   equal t?

   [handwritten: B]

   (A) 1
   (B) 2
   (C) 4
   (D) 9
   (E) 25

   [handwritten: $t = 1$ $x = 6$ $6-3=3$]
   [handwritten: $y = 3$ $1^6 = t^3$]
   [handwritten: $4-1$ $p=1$ $2^6 = t^3$]
   [handwritten: $p=2$ $3^6 = t^3$]
   [handwritten: $p=3$]

10. If $\dfrac{4y}{k}$ is the cube of an integer greater than 1,

    and $k^2 = y$, what is the least possible value of y?

    (A) 1
    (B) 2
    (C) 4
    (D) 6
    (E) 27

    [handwritten: $\dfrac{4y}{k} = x^3 > 1$]
    [handwritten: $k^2 = y$]
    [handwritten: $y=1$ $\dfrac{4y}{1} = 4$ $k^2 = 1$ $k=1$]
    [handwritten: $y=2$ $k^2 = 2$ $k = \sqrt{2}$ $\dfrac{4(2)}{\sqrt{2}} = \dfrac{8}{\sqrt{2}}$]
    [handwritten: $y=4$ $k^2 = 4$ $k = 2$ $\dfrac{16}{2} = 8$ 2]

Answers and Explanations: Problem Set 11

Easy

1. **D** $t = -2$, and $(-2)^2 = 4$.

2. **B** Plug 25 in for r and solve:
$$25 + \sqrt{25} = s^2 - 6$$
$$30 = s^2 - 6$$
$$36 = s^2$$
$$6 = s$$

3. **D** $x = 3$, and $4^3 = 64$. How did we know $x = 3$? Just plug in— $3^2 = 9$, $3^3 = 27$. There you go.

Medium

4. **D** In this function, all you have to do is square the first thing in the parentheses and put it over the square of the second thing in the parentheses. So $(2 + y) = \dfrac{2^2}{y^2}$. And $(y + 1) = \dfrac{y^2}{1}$. Now multiply them. The y^2 cancels, so you get 2^2.

5. **C** Let's plug in. If $p = 1$, then $k = 1$. Cross out (B), (D), and (E). Try $p = 4$. Then the cube root of k is equal to 2, so $k = 8$. That works, too. Cross out (A). (On the SAT, if you cross out 4 answers, just pick what's left and keep going. Don't stop to wonder why.)

6. **B** Remember that you can multiply or divide what's under a square root sign and add or subtract when what's under the square root sign is the same. Begin by simplifying the denominator. $\dfrac{\sqrt{a} \bullet \sqrt{b}}{3\sqrt{a} - 2\sqrt{a}} = \dfrac{\sqrt{a} \bullet \sqrt{b}}{\sqrt{a}} = \sqrt{b}$.

7. **A** Remember to take this question apart using bite-size pieces. First, get rid of your denominator by multiplying both sides by x^2. Now, you have $8^{\frac{2}{3}} = 20x^{-3}x^2$. You know that when you multiply exponential terms that have the same base, you can just add the exponents, so that leaves you with $8^{\frac{2}{3}} = 20x^2$. When you have a negative exponent, just write the reciprocal and you lose the negative. So, we can rewrite this as $8^{\frac{2}{3}} = \dfrac{20}{x^{-1}}$, which is really just $8^{\frac{2}{3}} = \dfrac{20}{x}$. Now let's deal with that fractional exponent. The numerator is the power we are raising 8 to, and the denominator is the root we are reducing it to. Let's tackle the denominator first. The cube root of 8 is 2. The square of 2 is 4. Thus, $4 = \dfrac{20}{x}$ and $x = 5$.

Hard

8. **B** First, let's analyze our inequality. All the stuff to the right is less than zero, so a^3bc^6 is negative. Anything with an even exponent has to be positive, so we know c^6 is positive. That means in a^3b, one variable is positive and the other negative. Let's go to the Roman numerals. We know I is *not* true, because either a or b is negative and the other positive. Cross out (A) and (D). Hey! II is just what we're looking for! Cross out (C). Now let's look at III. We know ab is negative—but we don't know a thing about c. We know that c^6 is positive, but c could be positive or negative. So cross out (E).

   This question is very difficult—you could plug numbers in, but in a question like this, they only get in the way. Your only concern is the sign of the variables.

9. **B** Let's try plugging in the answer choices for t and see which works. If $t = 1$, can we find values for p, x, and y that make the equations $x - y = 3$ and $p^x = 1^y$ true? Sure, if $p = 1$, $x = 4$, and $y = 1$. So we can eliminate choice (A). How about if we plug in $t = 2$? Now we've got some difficulty, so let's skip that one for now. Try plugging in $t = 4$. Can we make the equation true? Sure, if $p = 2$, $x = 6$, and $y = 3$. We can also make $t = 9$, if $p = 3$, $x = 6$, and $y = 3$. This allows us to eliminate (C) and (D). Likewise we can eliminate (E), since t could be 25 if $p = 5$, $x = 6$, and $y = 3$. So the answer must be (B).

10. **C** Plug in the answer choices. Since the question asks for the least possible value, start with (A). If $y = 1$, $k = 1$. $\dfrac{4(1)}{1} = 4$, which isn't a cube. Cross off (A). (B): If $y = 2$, then $k = \sqrt{2}$. Forget it, you don't have an integer. (C): If $y = 4$, then $k = 2$. $\dfrac{4(4)}{2} = 8$, which is the cube of 2. That was pretty painless, wasn't it?

PROBLEM SET 12: EQUATIONS: SIMPLE, POLYNOMIAL, QUADRATIC, AND SIMULTANEOUS

EASY

1. If $x^2 = \sqrt{y} + 2$, and $y = 4$, then $x =$

   (A) 2
   (B) 3
   (C) 4
   (D) 8
   (E) 36

2. If $60 = (7 + 8)(x - 2)$, then $x =$

   (A) 15
   (B) 10
   (C) 9
   (D) 7
   (E) 6

3. If $4x - 2y = 10$, and $7x + 2y = 23$, what is the value of x?

   (A) $\dfrac{1}{3}$

   (B) 1

   (C) 3

   (D) 13

   (E) 14

MEDIUM

4. If $\dfrac{x+2}{3} = \dfrac{(x+2)^2}{15}$, what is one possible value of x?

   (A) −1
   (B) 0
   (C) 1
   (D) 2
   (E) 3

5. For their science homework, Brenda and Dylan calculated the volume of air that filled a basketball. If the formula for the volume of a sphere is $V = \frac{4}{3}\pi r^3$, and the diameter of the basketball was 6, what was the volume of the air inside the basketball?

(A) 4π
(B) 14π
(C) 32π
(D) 36π
(E) 72π

6. If $ab = 6c$, and $\frac{c}{a} = \frac{b}{d}$, what is $\frac{d}{2}$?

(A) 3

(B) 6

(C) 12

(D) $\frac{a}{b}$

(E) $\frac{ab}{c}$

7. On a certain test, Radeesh earned 2 points for every correct answer and lost 1 point for every incorrect answer. If he answered all 30 questions on the test and received a score of 51, how many questions did Radeesh answer *incorrectly*?

(A) 3
(B) 7
(C) 15
(D) 21
(E) 24

Hard

8. If b is an integer, and $x^2 + bx - 30 = 0$, which of the following CANNOT be the value of b?

(A) 1
(B) 6
(C) 7
(D) 13
(E) 29

9. Twelve baseball cards were sold at an average price of $3 a card. If some of the cards cost $5 each and the rest cost $2 each, how many $5 cards were sold?

(A) 2
(B) 4
(C) 6
(D) 8
(E) 10

10. If $\dfrac{a}{b} + a = 6$, what is the value of

$$\sqrt{\dfrac{a + ab - 2b}{b}} \, ?$$

(A) 2

(B) $\sqrt{6}$

(C) 3

(D) 4

(E) $\sqrt{10}$

Answers and Explanations: Problem Set 12

Easy

1. **A** The question gives you $y = 4$, so plug it in.

   $x^2 = \sqrt{4} + 2$

   $x^2 = 2 + 2$

   $x^2 = 4$

   $x = 2$

2. **E** Plug in the answer choices. Try (C) first: $(15)(9 - 2) = (15)(7) = 105$. It should equal 60, so we need a much smaller number. Try (E): $(15)(6 - 2) = (15)(4) = 60$. It works. Or you could solve the equation algebraically:

   $60 = 15(x - 2)$

   $60 = 15x - 30$

   $90 = 15x$

   $6 = x$

3. **C** Stack 'em and add:

   $4x - 2y = 10$

   $7x + 2y = 23$

   $11x = 33$

   $x = 3$

Medium

4. **E** Let's plug in the answer choices, starting with choice (C). This gives

   you $\dfrac{1+2}{3} = \dfrac{(1+2)^2}{15}$, which is $\dfrac{5}{3} = \dfrac{25}{15}$. Well, that didn't work. (E) gives

   you $\dfrac{3+2}{3} = \dfrac{(3+2)^2}{15} \cdot \dfrac{5}{3} = \dfrac{25}{15}$ and $\dfrac{5}{3} = \dfrac{5}{3}$. That works. If you solve this

   algebraically, you get $x = 3$ or -2, and who needs to waste time getting

   an answer that isn't even one of the choices? You don't.

5. **D** Don't worry—you weren't supposed to know this formula. That's why they gave it to you, so don't get freaked out. Just use the information in the question to solve for V. If the diameter of the basketball was 6, the radius was 3:

$$V = \frac{4}{3}\pi r^3, \text{ so } V = \frac{4}{3}\pi(3^3) = \frac{4}{3}\pi(27) = 36\pi.$$

You may see some totally unfamiliar formula on the test—physics, for instance—but you don't have to understand the formula or know anything about it. All you have to do is substitute in any value they give you and solve for the variable they ask for.

6. **A** Try plugging in $a = 4$, $b = 3$, and $c = 2$. d comes out to 6, and $\frac{6}{2}$ is 3. None of the other answer choices works, so (A) must be the right answer.

7. **A** Let's plug in the answer choices. If Radeesh got 2 points for every right answer, and the test had 30 questions, the top score was 60. If he got a 51, he did pretty well, so start with (A). (Remember, the answer choices represent the number of questions he answered incorrectly.) If he missed 3, then he got 27 right. $27 \times 2 = 54$. Subtract 3 for 3 wrong answers, and you get 51. Fabulous.

   [Don't worry if you didn't see which answer to start with. If you started with (C), it gave you way too many wrong answers, didn't it? So cross off (C), (D), and (E) and you've only got 2 left to try.]

HARD

8. **B** Once again, we can plug in the answer choices. Start with (C). That makes the equation $x^2 + 7x - 30 = 0$. Can you factor that? Sure—it's $(x + 10)(x - 3)$. Cross out (C). Now try (B), because 6 is an easy number to work with. (It's better than 13 and 29, isn't it?) Try factoring $x^2 + 6x - 30$. You can't. Since you're looking for the answer that CANNOT be k, (B) is correct.

9. **B** This is ugly, but we can plug in the answer choices to make it much easier. Try (C) first: If 6 cards worth $5 were sold, that's a total of $30. If the total sold was $12, that leaves 6 cards worth $2, for a total of $12. To get the average cost per card, divide the total cost by the number of cards: $42 ÷ 12 isn't $3. Try something smaller: (B) gives you 4 cards at $5, for a total of $20, and 8 cards at $2 for a total of $16. That adds up to $36. Now for the average: $36 ÷ 12 = $3. The "math" way to solve this would be to write simultaneous equations: $x + y = 12$ and $5x + 2y = 3(x + y)$. What's wrong with doing it that way? Well, first you have to write not one but two equations correctly. Then you have to solve them. All of that takes too much time and allows too many opportunities for mistakes.

10. A This is a very difficult question. Since there are 2 variables and the equation is equal to a specific number, we can't plug in (as you may have found out). Since the answer choices are equal to that ugly square root with 2 variables, we can't plug in the answer choices, either. Since there aren't 2 equations, we can't do simultaneous equations. So we're stuck with algebra.

Look at the square root we're solving for. Ignore the square root sign for a minute, and do the division underneath.

$$\frac{a+ab-2b}{b} = \frac{a}{b}+\frac{ab}{b}-\frac{2b}{b} = \frac{a}{b}+a-2.$$

Now look back at the equation: If $\frac{a}{b}+a = 6$, you can substitute 6 for that part, which leaves you with $\sqrt{4}$, which equals 2.

If you didn't get this question right, don't sweat it unless you're aiming for a 700 or higher. Even then, this would be a good problem to leave blank.

PROBLEM SET 13: LINES, ANGLES, AND COORDINATES

EASY

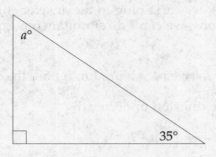

1. In the figure above, $3a - a =$

    (A) 40
    (B) 55
    (C) 90
    (D) 110
    (E) 165

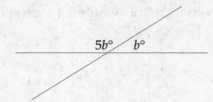

2. In the figure above, $b =$

    (A) 20
    (B) 30
    (C) 40
    (D) 45
    (E) 180

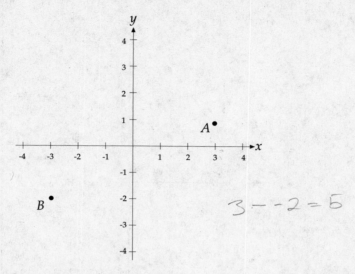

3 − −2 = 5

3. The x-coordinate of Point A minus the y-coordinate of Point B equals

(A) −2
(B) −1
(C) 0
(D) 3
(E) 5

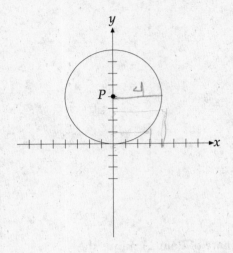

4. Point *P* is the center of circle *Q*, which has a

    radius of 4. Which of the following points lies

    on circle *Q*?

    (A) (4, 0)
    (B) (0, 4)
    (C) (–4, 4)
    (D) (3, 1)
    (E) (4, 3)

5. In the rectangle above, $p + q - r =$ $p+q=90-r=0$

    (A) 0
    (B) 15
    (C) 26
    (D) 35
    (E) 50

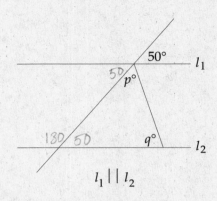

$l_1 \parallel l_2$

Note: Figure not drawn to scale.

6. In the figure above, $p + q =$

    (A) 180
    (B) 150
    (C) 130
    (D) 90
    (E) 70

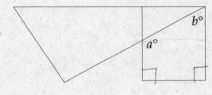

$a = 130$
$b = 45$
175

$a + b = 180$

7. The figure above is formed by a triangle
    overlapping a rectangle. What does
    $a + b$ equal?

    (A) 80
    (B) 90
    (C) 150
    (D) 180
    (E) 270

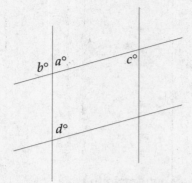

Note: Figure not drawn to scale.

8. Which of the following statements must be true?

   I. $a + b < 180$
   II. $a + d = 180$
   III. $a + d > 180$

   (A) None
   (B) I only
   (C) II only
   (D) I and II only
   (E) II and II only

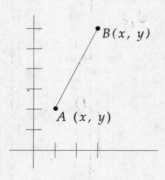

$$\frac{6-2}{3-1} = \frac{4}{2} = 2$$

9. If the coordinates of Point A are $(1, 2)$, what is the slope of line AB?

   (A) -3

   (B) -2

   (C) $\dfrac{1}{2}$

   (D) 2

   (E) 3

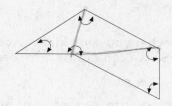

10. What is the total number of degrees of the marked angles?

(A) 180
(B) 270
(C) 360
(D) 540
(E) 720

ANSWERS AND EXPLANATIONS: PROBLEM SET 13

EASY

1. **D** A triangle has 180°. So $90 + 35 + a = 180$, and $a = 55$. Plug that into the equation and get $3(55) - 55 = 110$.

2. **B** $5b$ and b lie on a straight line, so $5b + b = 180$ and $b = 30$.

3. **E** The x-coordinate of Point A is 3, and the y-coordinate of Point B is -2. So $3 - (-2) = 5$.

MEDIUM

4. **C** Just plot the points and see which one falls on the circle.

5. **A** As always, mark whatever info you can on your diagram: $r = 90$, and the bottom angle is also 90, because this is a rectangle. $p + q = 90$, because they are the two remaining angles in a right triangle. That means $p + q - r = 0$.

6. **C** Again, mark info on the diagram. The unmarked angle of the triangle is 50°, so $50 + p + q = 180$ and $p + q = 130°$. (You can't figure out what p and q are individually, but the question doesn't ask you to.)

7. **D** Estimate first. a is around 130 and b is bigger than 45, so $a + b$ should be a little bigger than 175. Pick (D) and keep cruising. To figure the angles exactly, ignore the triangle and look at the quadrilateral in the bottom half of the rectangle. The angles are $a + b + 90 + 90$. Since a quadrilateral has 360°, $a + b = 180$.

HARD

8. **A** It's important to realize what you *don't* know: Are any of these lines parallel? *We don't know.* So we can't draw any conclusions at all. None. Zero, zip, nada.

9. **D** Mark the points on your diagram, so that (x, y) is $(1, 2)$. That makes $(3x, 3y) = (3, 6)$. The slope is $\dfrac{6-2}{3-1} = \dfrac{4}{2} = 2.$

10. **D** Estimate first and see what you can cross out. Since you have two angles that are bigger than 90 and one angle that's bigger than 180, you should be able at least to cross out (A), (B), and (C). To figure out the exact number of degrees, divide the figure into three triangles:

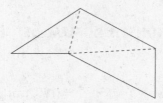

The total degrees will be $180 \times 3 = 540.$

PROBLEM SET 14: TRIANGLES

EASY

1. If the area of the triangle above is 6, what is its perimeter?

    (A) 8
    (B) 11
    (C) 12
    (D) 15
    (E) 16

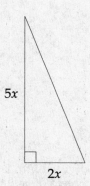

2. If $x = 3$, what is the area of the triangle above?

    (A) 10
    (B) 12
    (C) 21
    (D) 30
    (E) 45

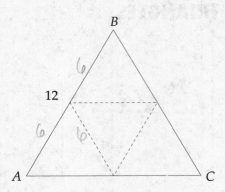

3. If equilateral triangle *ABC* is cut by three lines, as shown, to form four equilateral triangles of equal area, what is the length of a side of 1 of the smaller triangles?

(A) 3
(B) 4
(C) 5
(D) 6
(E) 8

MEDIUM

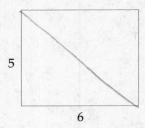

4. If the rectangle above is divided into 2 triangles, then the sum of the perimeters of *both* triangles is

(A) equal to 30
(B) less than 30
(C) equal to 32
(D) equal to 34
(E) greater than 34

5. A movie theater is 3 blocks due north of a supermarket, and a beauty parlor is 4 blocks due east of the movie theater. How many blocks long is the street that runs directly from the supermarket to the beauty parlor?

(A) 2.5
(B) 3
(C) 4
(D) 5
(E) 7

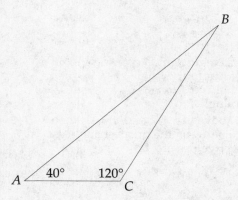

6. In triangle *ABC* above, if line *CD* (not shown) bisects *AB*, which of the following must be true?

  I. $DB > BC$
 II. $AD = DB$
III. $AB > BC$

(A) I only
(B) II only
(C) III only
(D) I and II only
(E) II and III only

HARD

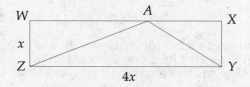

7. In the figure above, what is the area of triangle *YAZ*?

(A) $3x$
(B) x^2
(C) $5x$
(D) $2x^2$
(E) $4x^2$

8. If a triangle has vertices of (–1, 5), (–1, –3), and (5, –3), then the perimeter of the triangle is

(A) 8
(B) 10
(C) 15
(D) 24
(E) 30

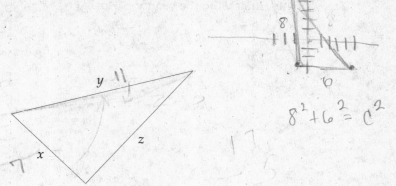

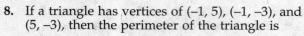

9. In the figure above, if $x = 7$ and $y = 11$, then the difference between the greatest and least possible integer values of z is

(A) 11
(B) 12
(C) 13
(D) 14
(E) 15

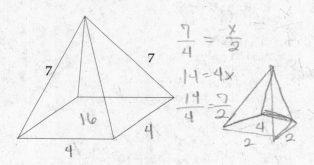

10. The pyramid above has a square base with an area of 16. If the top of the pyramid is cut off to make a smaller pyramid whose base has an area of 4, then the length of the edge from the vertex to the new base is

(A) $\dfrac{7}{4}$

(B) 2

(C) $\dfrac{7}{2}$

(D) 4

(E) 5

ANSWERS AND EXPLANATIONS: PROBLEM SET 14

EASY

1. **C** Several ways to get this question: You could recognize that it's a Pythagorean triple (3:4:5), which would give you the length of the unmarked leg. Or you could set up the following equation:

$$a = \frac{1}{2}bh$$

$\frac{1}{2}b(4) = 6$, so $2b = 6$ and $b = 3$. All we did was substitute the height and the area, both of which are given in the problem, into the formula for the area of a triangle.

2. **E** If $x = 3$, then the base of the triangle is 6 and the height is 15. That would mean the area is $\frac{1}{2}(6)(15) = 45$.

3. **D** Here's what your picture should look like:

Each of our 3 lines bisected 2 sides of the big triangle, so each side is 6. (Don't forget to estimate.)

MEDIUM

4. **E** First draw a diagonal, which divides the rectangle into 2 triangles. Now estimate: How long does that diagonal look? It's definitely longer than 6—so the perimeter of each triangle must be bigger than 17, so both perimeters must be greater than 34. Cross out (A), (B), and (C). Now be more precise. The diagonal looks like it's about 8, wouldn't you say? So the perimeter of 1 triangle is around 19, and the perimeter of both is around 38. Pick (D). (To figure this exactly, you have to use the Pythagorean theorem: $5^2 + 6^2 = c^2$. So $c^2 = \sqrt{61}$, which is a little less than 8.)

5. **D** Draw a little map, which should look like this:

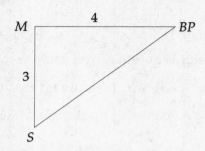

Now you have a 3:4:5 right triangle, so the street from the supermarket to the beauty parlor is 5 blocks long.

6. **E** Draw a line from C that bisects AB. It should look like this:

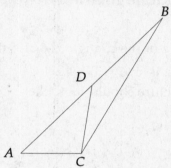

Now you can estimate. *DB* isn't longer than *BC*, is it? Cross out (A) and (D). Is *AD* longer than *DC*? Yes, (D) is the midpoint of *AB*, remember? Cross out (C). Is *AB* longer than *BC*? Definitely, so the answer is (E). The rule for triangles is that the longest leg is opposite the widest angle; the shortest leg is opposite the smallest angle. (Draw yourself a few triangles and you'll see it works.)

HARD

7. **D** Let's plug in. If $x = 2$, then *ZY* is 8 and *WZ* is 2. (Write that on your diagram.) To get the area of *YAZ*, notice that *WZ* is the height of the triangle, so $\frac{1}{2}(8)(2) = 8$. Plug 2 back into the answer choices, and (D) is $2(2^2) = 8$.

8. **D** Make yourself a grid so you can see what you're doing. It should look like this:

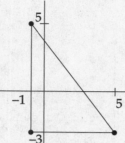

Obviously your drawing won't be exactly to scale, but don't worry about it. Now count up the distance of the sides. From (−1, −3) to (5, −3) is 6 units. From (−1, −3) to (−1, 5) is 8 units. To figure out the distance from (−1, 5) to (5, −3), either estimate or use the Pythagorean theorem. It's a 6:8:10 right triangle, so that distance is 10 and the perimeter is 6 + 8 + 10 = 24.

9. **B** Here's the rule: The sum of any two sides of a triangle must be more than the third side. So if we already have sides of 7 and 11, the longest the third side could be is a little less than 18. Since the third side has to be an integer, the longest it could be is 17. Now for the shortest possible length of the third side: 11 − 7 = 4, so the third side has to be an integer bigger than 4—that's 5. So the difference between the greatest possible and the least possible is 17 − 5 = 12.

10. **C** If the area of the base is 16, the side of the base is 4. (Don't forget that the base is square.) If we want our new pyramid to have a base with an area of 4, then the new side will be 2. Any face of the original pyramid will be similar to any face of the new pyramid because all the angles stay the same. Since the triangles are similar, the legs are in proportion. If the base goes from 4 to 2, we cut it in half, so the side goes from 7 to $\frac{7}{2}$. Or you could set up a proportion: $\frac{4}{7} = \frac{2}{x}$, with $\frac{4}{7}$ as the original pyramid's base-to-edge and $\frac{2}{x}$ as the smaller pyramid's base-to-edge.

TIP:
On problems like this that deal with complex shapes, give yourself plenty of time to visualize the problem before trying to solve it.

PROBLEM SET 15: CIRCLES

EASY

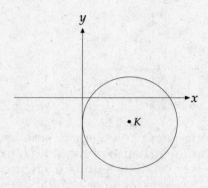

1. Point *K* is the center of the circle above, and the coordinates of Point *K* are (2, –1). What is the area of the circle?

   (A) π
   (B) 2π
   (C) 4π
   (D) 6π
   (E) 8π

2. Circle *P* has a radius of 7, and Circle *R* has a diameter of 8. The circumference of Circle *P* is how much greater than the circumference of Circle *R*?

   (A) π
   (B) 6π
   (C) 8π
   (D) 16π
   (E) 33π

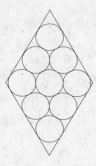

3. Nine circular tiles are arranged as above as part of a pattern in a floor design. Each tile has a diameter of 1 inch. If the group of 9 tiles is enclosed by a diamond-shaped border that lies tangent to the exterior tiles, what is the total length, in inches, of the border?

(A) 4
(B) 6
(C) 8
(D) 9
(E) 12

MEDIUM

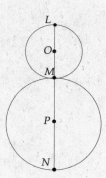

4. In the figure above, LM is $\frac{1}{3}$ of LN. If the radius of the circle with center P is 6, what is the area of the circle with center O?

(A) 4π
(B) 9π
(C) 12π
(D) 18π
(E) 36π

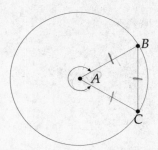

5. In the figure above, the circle has center A, and $BC = AB$. What is the degree measure of the marked angle?

(A) 60°
(B) 180°
(C) 270°
(D) 300°
(E) 340°

6. What is the greatest number of distinct regions that could be formed by a circle overlapped by a triangle?

(A) 3
(B) 4
(C) 6
(D) 7
(E) 8

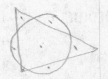

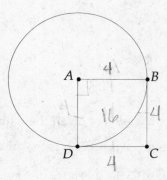

$$\frac{8\pi}{4} = 2\pi$$

$C = 2\pi(4)$

$\frac{8\pi}{4} = 2\pi$

7. Points D and B lie on the circle above with center A. If square $ABCD$ has an area of 16, what is the length of arc BD?

(A) 2π
(B) 4
(C) 8
(D) 4π
(E) 8π

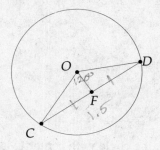

8. In the figure above, what is the circumference of the circle with center *O*, if *COD* is 120° and *OF* bisects *CD* and has a length of 1.5?

(A) $\dfrac{2\pi}{3}$

(B) $\dfrac{3\pi}{2}$

(C) 3π

(D) 6π

(E) 9π

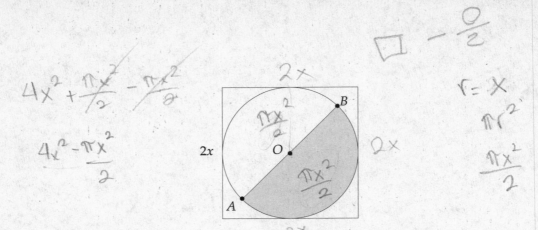

2x

$4x^2 + \dfrac{\pi x^2}{2} - \dfrac{\pi x^2}{2}$

$\dfrac{4x^2 - \pi x^2}{2}$

$\square - \dfrac{O}{2}$

$r = x$

πr^2

$\dfrac{\pi x^2}{2}$

9. In the figure above, the circle with center O is inscribed in a square with sides of $2x$. If AB is a diameter of the circle, then in terms of x, what is the total area of the unshaded regions?

(A) $4x^2 + \pi x^2$

(B) $4x + \dfrac{\pi x^2}{2}$

(C) $4x^2 - \dfrac{\pi x^2}{2}$

(D) $4x^2 - \pi x$

(E) $2x - \dfrac{\pi x^2}{2}$

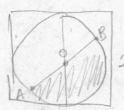

2x

$AB = 2x$ $r = x$

$A = \pi r^2$

$A = \pi x^2$

$(2x)^2 - \dfrac{\pi x^2}{2}$

10. In a certain machine, a gear makes 12 revolutions per minute. If the circumference of the gear is 3π inches, approximately how many *feet* will the gear turn in an hour?

(A)   6,782
(B)   565
(C)   113
(D)   108
(E)   9

ANSWERS AND EXPLANATIONS: PROBLEM SET 15

EASY

1. **C** Count up the units of the radius—it's 2. Then use the formula for area of a circle: $\pi r^2 = \pi(2^2) = 4\pi$.

2. **B** The circumference of Circle P is $2\pi r = 2\pi(7) = 14\pi$. The circumference of Circle R is $2\pi r = 2\pi(4) = 8\pi$. Now just subtract. If you picked (E), you calculated area instead of circumference.

3. **E** Draw the diamond-shaped border around the circles. Write the diameter of a circle on your diagram, too. Each side of the border is 3 diameters, or 3 inches—so all four sides will have $4 \times 3 = 12$ inches.

MEDIUM

4. **B** Write in 6 by the radius of the bigger circle. That makes the diameter of the bigger circle 12. If LM (the diameter of the smaller circle) is $\frac{1}{3}$ the length of LN, the equation is $\left(\frac{1}{3}\right)(12 + x) = x$. $4 = x - \frac{x}{3}$, and $x = 6$. (You don't have to write an equation. You could estimate and try some numbers. Doesn't LM look like it's about half of MN? It is.) If the diameter of the smaller circle is 6, then its radius is 3 and its area is 9π.

5. **D** Estimate first. The marked angle is way more than 180—in fact, it's not that far from 360. Cross out (A) and (B). You know $AC = AB$ because they're both radii. That means $BC = AB = AC$, and that triangle is equilateral. So angle BAC is 60°. Subtract that from 360 and you're in business. (Even if all you could do was estimate, go ahead and take a guess.)

6. **D** Draw a few diagrams and see how many regions you can come up with. Here's what the diagram should look like:

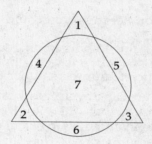

7. **A** If the square has an area of 16, then the side of the square is 4. Write that on your diagram. Now you know the radius of the circle is also 4, so the circumference is 8π. Angle BAD has 90°, since it's a corner of the square. And since 90 is $\frac{1}{4}$ of 360, arc BD is $\frac{1}{4}$ of the circumference. (Pretty cool, huh?) So arc BD is $\left(\frac{1}{4}\right)(8\pi)$, or 2π. If you estimated first, as we hope you did, you could have crossed out (D) and (E), and maybe even (C).

HARD

8. **D** Write the info on your diagram. If *OF* bisects *CD*, it also bisects angle *COD*, making two 60° angles. Now there are two 30:60:90 triangles. If the shortest leg of one of those triangles is 1.5, then the hypotenuse is 2 × 1.5, or 3. Aha! That distance is also the radius of the circle, so the circumference is 6π.

9. **C** This one's pretty ugly. To get the unshaded part of the square, we're going to get the area of the whole square and then subtract the shaded part. If the side of the square is 2*x*, then the area is $4x^2$. Cross out (E). The diameter of the circle is equal to the side of the square, even if the diagram shows it tipped to one side. The radius, then, is half the side of the square, or *x*. The area of the whole circle is πx^2, and the area of the shaded semicircle is $\dfrac{\pi x^2}{2}$. Now all we have to do is subtract that shaded area from the area of the square, and we get $4x^2 - \dfrac{\pi x^2}{2}$.

If all those *x*s made you nervous, you could of course plug in something simple for *x*, like 2. It helps to plug in on geometry because it's easier to think of lengths as concrete numbers rather than as variables.

10. **B** First make π = 3, so the gear travels 9 inches per revolution. If it makes 12 revolutions per minute, that's 12 × 9 = 108 inches per minute, which is 108 × 60 = 6,480 inches in an hour. To calculate feet, simply divide by 12, and you get 540. Did you pick (A)? They asked for feet, my friend, not inches. *Read carefully.*

> **TIP:**
> One more thing: Circle questions tend to appear most often in the late-medium and hard questions.

PROBLEM SET 16: QUADRILATERALS, BOXES, AND CANS

EASY

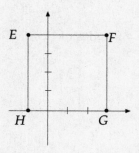

1. The coordinates of Point *E* are (−1, 4), and the coordinates of Point *H* are (−1, 0). If *EFGH* is a square, what are the coordinates of Point *F*?

   (A) (3, 4)
   (B) (3, 0)
   (C) (3, 5)
   (D) (4, 1)
   (E) (4, −1)

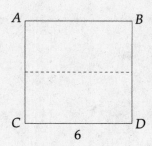

2. The square above is folded on the dotted line so that *A* is directly on top of *C*. If the square is folded again so that *B* is on top of *C*, what is the length of the side of the new square?

   (A) 2

   (B) 3

   (C) $3\sqrt{2}$

   (D) 4

   (E) $3\sqrt{3}$

6

2

3. How many squares with sides of 1 could fit into the rectangle above?

(A) 3
(B) 4
(C) 6
(D) 9
(E) 12

MEDIUM

4. The area of Rectangle *K* is three times the area of Rectangle *Q*. The area of Rectangle *Q* is twice the area of Rectangle *P*. If the area of Rectangle *Q* is 4, what is the difference between the area of Rectangle *K* and Rectangle *P*?

(A) 12
(B) 10
(C) 8
(D) 6
(E) 2

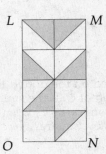

5. Rectangle *LMNO* is divided into 8 square sections. If the area of *LMNO* is 24, what is the total area of the shaded regions?

(A) 12
(B) 9
(C) 8
(D) 6
(E) 2

$3x$

7

Note: Figure not drawn to scale.

6. If the area of the rectangle above is 42, what is the value of x^2?

(A) 24
(B) 21
(C) 6
(D) 4
(E) 2

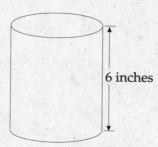

6 inches

7. In the figure above, the radius of the base of the cylinder is half its height. What is the volume of the cylinder in cubic inches?

(A) 9 π
(B) 15 π
(C) 18 π
(D) 36 π
(E) 54 π

HARD

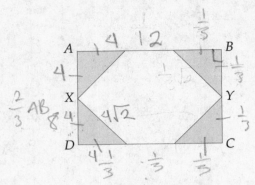

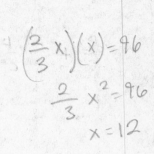

8. The area of rectangle $ABCD$ is 96, and

   $AD = \dfrac{2}{3}(AB)$. Points X and Y are midpoints

   of AD and BC, respectively. If the 4 shaded

   triangles are isosceles, what is the perimeter of

   the unshaded hexagon?

   (A) 16
   (B) $8 + 6\sqrt{2}$
   (C) 24
   (D) $8 + 16\sqrt{2}$
   (E) $16 + 24\sqrt{2}$

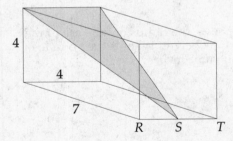

9. In the figure above, S is the midpoint of RT.
   What is the area of the shaded triangle?

   (A) 14
   (B) 16
   (C) $2\sqrt{65}$
   (D) 18
   (E) $4\sqrt{6}$

10. A ball with a volume of 18 cubic inches is dropped into an aquarium that is partially filled with water. If the base of the aquarium measures 12 inches by 6 inches, how many inches will the level of water rise after the ball is submerged?

(A) $\frac{1}{4}$ inches

(B) $\frac{1}{2}$ inches

(C) 1 inches

(D) 4 inches

(E) 6 inches

Answers and Explanations: Problem Set 16

Easy

1. **A** Write the coordinates of E and H on your diagram. What's the distance between E and H? It's 4, so F is 4 units to the right of E. (The figure is a square.) Since the x-coordinate of E is -1, four units to the right of E is 3. And since F has the same y-coordinate as E, the coordinates of F are (3, 4).

2. **B** After the first fold, the figure is a rectangle that measures 6 by 3. If it is then folded again, in half, it will be a square again, with sides of 3. This is a visual perception question—if you had trouble with it, cut a square piece of paper and fold it twice, following the directions in the question, and see what happens.

3. **E** Drawing on the diagram could help. How many sides of 1 can fit along the long edge of the rectangle? 6. And how many rows will fit along the short edge? 2. Now just multiply $6 \times 2 = 12$. Or draw them in and count them up.

MEDIUM

4. **B** If the area of Q is 4, then the area of P is 2 and the area of K is 12. So the difference between the areas of K and P is $12 - 2 = 10$. Don't bother writing equations to solve this problem—it's a waste of time. Just use the given number (4), and figure out the other areas one at a time.

5. **B** If the total area is 24, and there are 8 sections, then each section has an area of 3. The 6 triangles are half-sections, so each triangle has an area of 1.5. And $1.5 \times 6 = 9$. If you estimate, you should be able to cross out (E), at least. Or just look at the diagram and see that a total of 3 out of the 8 squares are shaded: $\dfrac{3}{8} \cdot \dfrac{24}{1} = 9$.

6. **D** $7 \times 3x = 42$, so $21x = 42$ and $x = 2$. But don't pick (E)! One last thing— the question asks for x^2, so $2^2 = 4$. (A lot of SAT questions are testing your ability to follow directions, so make sure you reread the question carefully before bubbling in your final answer.)

7. **E** If the radius is half the height, then the radius is 3. To get the volume of a cylinder, multiply the area of the base times the height—in this case, $\pi(3^2) \times 6 = 54\pi$.

HARD

8. **D** First calculate the dimensions of the rectangle. If the area is 96 and the width is $\dfrac{2}{3}$ of the height, your equation is $x \bullet \left(\dfrac{2}{3}\right)x = 96$. $\dfrac{2x^2}{3} = 96$, $x^2 = 144$, and $x = 12$. So the long side is 12 and the short side is $\dfrac{2}{3}$ of 12, or 8. If X and Y are midpoints, then AX, XD, BY, and YC all equal 4. Since the triangles are isosceles, the legs of the triangles (not the hypotenuses) are also 4. Here's what we have so far:

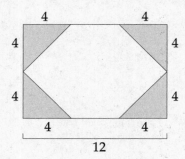

The unmarked piece of the long side of the rectangle is also 4, since the side is 12 altogether. Since we have isosceles *right* triangles, the hypotenuses are $4\sqrt{2}$. Now add it all up: The 4 hypotenuses would be $4(4\sqrt{2}) = 16\sqrt{2}$, and the sides of the hexagon that lie along the rectangle would be $2(4) = 8$. So the total perimeter of the hexagon is $8 + 16\sqrt{2}$.

9. **C** Part of this problem is easy—the base of the triangle is 4. Now for the hard part: Imagine drawing an altitude of the triangle from the center of the base all the way to the tip. That's the same as drawing a diagonal of the side of the face measuring 4 by 7. So to calculate the altitude of the triangle, use the Pythagorean theorem to find the hypotenuse of the right triangle formed by drawing a diagonal on the side of the box. $4^2 + 7^2 = c^2$, $16 + 49 = c^2$, $c = \sqrt{65}$. That means the area of the shaded triangle is $\frac{1}{2}(4)(\sqrt{65}) = 2\sqrt{65}$.

10. **A** The important concept here is that the base of the aquarium remains constant and the height of the water is *not* constant. (The problem doesn't tell you the height of the aquarium because it doesn't matter.) If the base is 12 by 6, then its area is 72. If the ball has a volume of 18, then it will make the water rise $\frac{1}{4}$ inch, because $72 \times \frac{1}{4} = 18$.

To clarify: Let's say the water in the aquarium was 1 inch deep. Then the volume of water would be $l \times w \times h = 12 \times 6 \times 1 = 72$. If we drop in a ball with a volume of 18, then the new volume of the water would be 72 (new height) = 72 + 18, and the new height = $1\frac{1}{4}$. So the water level went from 1 to $1\frac{1}{4}$ inches deep.

PROBLEM SET 17: FUNCTIONS

Easy

1. If $f(2) = 5$ and $f(3) = 10$, which of the following could be $f(x)$?

   (A) $f(x) = 2x + 1$
   (B) $f(x) = 3x - 1$
   (C) $f(x) = 3x + 1$
   (D) $f(x) = x^2 - 1$
   (E) $f(x) = x^2 + 1$

2. If $f(x) = (x + 5)^2 + 8$, then what is the sum of the values of x for which $f(x) = 12$?

   (A) −10
   (B) −7
   (C) 10
   (D) 20
   (E) 297

3. If $f(x) = 2x + 1$ and $f(a) = 2$, what is the value of a?

   (A) −2

   (B) $-\dfrac{1}{2}$

   (C) $\dfrac{1}{2}$

   (D) 2

   (E) 5

Medium

4. If $f(x) = \dfrac{\sqrt{x}}{4}$, and $g(x) = \sqrt{x} + 5$, what is $f(g(16))$?

   (A) $\dfrac{3}{4}$

   (B) $\dfrac{\sqrt{21}}{4}$

   (C) 1

   (D) $\dfrac{9}{4}$

   (E) 4

5. If $f(1) = 2$ and $f(n + 1) = (f(n))^2$, what is the value of $f(4)$?

(A)   4
(B)   16
(C)   64
(D)   256
(E) 65,536

6. What is the value of $f(f(7))$ if $f(x) = 3x - 11$?

(A) –8
(B) 10
(C) 19
(D) 33
(E) 40

7. A backpacker found that the weight of her backpack determined the distance that she could comfortably hike. The heavier her pack, the shorter the distance she could comfortably hike. If w is the weight of her pack in pounds and D is the distance in miles that she can comfortably hike, which of the following could express the relationship of w and D?

(A) $D(w) = \dfrac{w^2}{400}$

(B) $D(w) = 400w$

(C) $D(w) = \dfrac{400}{w}$

(D) $D(w) = w - 400$

(E) $D(w) = 400\sqrt{w}$

Hard

8. The change in temperature is a function of the change in altitude in such a way that as the altitude increases, so does the change in the temperature. For example, a gain of 1,980 feet causes a 6°F change in temperature. If a represents the altitude gained, in feet, and T represents the temperature change in °F, which of the following could be the relationship of a and T?

(A) $T(a) = \dfrac{a}{330}$

(B) $T(a) = a - 330$

(C) $T(a) = \dfrac{330}{a}$

(D) $T(a) = 330 - a$

(E) $T(a) = 330a$

9. If $f(1) = 5$ and $f(n + 1) = 2(f(n)) - 6$, what is the value of $f(3)$?

(A) −2
(B) 2
(C) 4
(D) 6
(E) 15

10. Let $f(x)$ be defined as the least integer greater than $\dfrac{x}{5}$. Let $g(x)$ be defined as the greatest integer less than $\dfrac{x}{5}$. What is the value of $g(18) + f(102)$?

(A) 21
(B) 22
(C) 23
(D) 24
(E) 25

Answers and Explanations: Problem Set 17

Easy

1. **E** Plug in 2 for x to see if the answer yields 5. Then, try 3 for x to see if the answer yields 10. For (A), does $2(2) + 1 = 5$? Yes. Does $2(3) + 1 = 10$? No, eliminate (A). For (B), does $3(2) - 1 = 5$? Yes. Does $3(3) - 1 = 10$? No, eliminate (B). For (C), does $3(2) + 1 = 5$? No, eliminate (C). For (D), does $(2)^2 - 1 = 5$? No, eliminate (D). For (E), does $(2)^2 + 1 = 5$? Yes. Does $(3)^2 + 1 = 10$? Yes; so, (E) is correct.

2. **A** In this case, plug in answer choices for the value of x, starting with answer (C). Plugging 10 in for x gives you $f(10) = (10 + 5)^2 + 8 = 233$. But you want $f(x) = 12$, so eliminate (C). Now try (B): $f(-7) = 12$, so this is the right answer. Alternatively, set $f(x) = 12$, and solve $12 = (x + 5)^2 + 8$.

3. **C** If $f(a) = 2a + 1$, and $f(a) = 2$, that means $2 = 2a + 1$. Subtract 1 from both sides to get $1 = 2a$. Divide both sides by 2 to find $a = \dfrac{1}{2}$.

Medium

4. **A** First, find $g(16) = \sqrt{16} + 5 = 4 + 5 = 9$. Next, find $f(9) = \dfrac{\sqrt{9}}{4} = \dfrac{3}{4}$.

5. **D** Take it one step at a time. Note that $f(2) = f(1 + 1)$. So, n is 1 in $f(n + 1)$. So, $f(2) = (f(1))^2 = (2)^2$. Next, note that $f(3) = f(2 + 1)$. So, n is 2 in $f(n + 1)$. So, $f(3) = (f(2))^2 = (4)^2 = 16$. Next, note that $f(4) = f(3 + 1)$. So, n is 3 in $f(n + 1)$. So, $f(4) = (f(3))^2 = (16)^2 = 256$.

6. **C** First, find the value of $f(7)$ by plugging in 7 for x to get $f(7) = 3(7) - 11 = 10$. Since you are looking for $f(f(7))$, and $f(7) = 10$, the next step is to find $f(10)$. To do this, plug in 10 for x to get $f(f(7)) = 3(10) - 11$, or 19.

7. **C** The relationship is the greater the weight, the shorter the distance. So, the correct function is one that yields a shorter D as you increase the w. Try plugging in 10 and 20 for w. The correct answer will have a smaller D for 20 than it does for 10. Only (C) decreases as you increase w. That is $\dfrac{400}{10} > \dfrac{400}{20}$.

HARD

8. **A** The relationship is the greater the time, the greater the height. So, the correct function is one that yields a greater H as you increase t. Try plugging in for t in the functions to see which one increases as t increases. So, try $t = 10$ and $t = 20$. Only (A) has a greater H for $t = 10$ than it does for $t = 20$. That is $\dfrac{1}{2}(10 - 7) > \dfrac{1}{2}(20 - 7)$.

9. **B** Break down the problem into pieces. First, $f(2) = f(1 + 1)$. Use 1 for n in $f(n + 1)$. So, $f(2) = 2(f(1)) - 6 = 2(5) - 6 = 10 - 6 = 4$. So, $f(2) = 4$. Now, let's repeat the process. $f(3) = f(2 + 1)$. So, n is 2 in $f(2 + 1)$. So, $f(3) = 2(f(2)) - 6 = 2(4) - 6 = 8 - 6 = 2$.

10. **D** This one requires some careful reading. The $g(18)$ will be the least integer greater than $\dfrac{18}{5}$, which is 4. The $f(102)$ will be the greatest integer less than $\dfrac{102}{5}$, which is 20. Now we add them together and get 24.

PROBLEM SET 18: CHARTS AND GRAPHS

EASY

	Original Price	Sale Price
Store *A*	$25	$20
Store *B*	$20	$15
Store *C*	$30	$25
Store *D*	$35	$30

1. The chart above shows the original and sale prices of a certain item at each of four different stores. Which of the following stores provides a discount of 20% or more on this item?

    I. Store *A*
    II. Store *B*
    III. Store C

    (A) I only
    (B) II only
    (C) III only
    (D) I and II only
    (E) I and III only

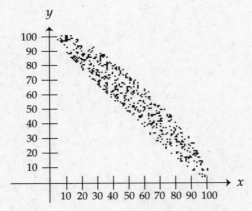

2. Which of the following is mostly likely the slope of the line of best fit for the scatterplot above?

    (A) −10
    (B) −1
    (C) 0
    (D) 1
    (E) 10

Daily Temperature (Fahrenheit)	Number of Campers per Week in Greenstone Park
60°	2,000
75°	2,500
85°	3,000
95°	2,250

3. According to the above chart, the relationship between the daily high temperature and the number of campers per week in Greenstone Park is best represented by which of the following graphs?

(A)

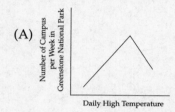

(B)

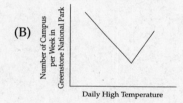

(C)

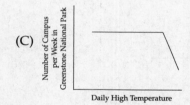

(D)

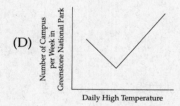

(E)

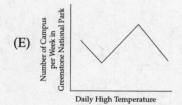

MEDIUM

4. If $f(x) = 4x + 2$, which of the following is the
    graph of $f(x)$?

    (A)

    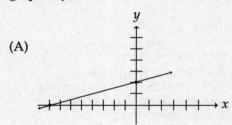

    (B)

    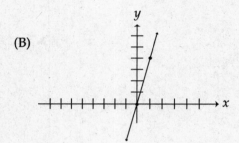

    (C)

    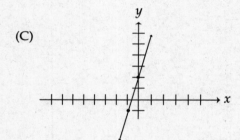

    (D)

    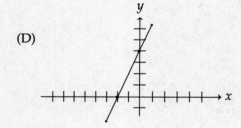

    (E)

    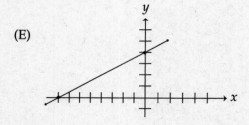

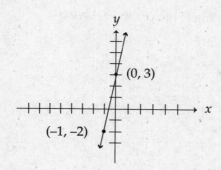

(0, 3)

(−1, −2)

5. If the graph above is that of $f(x)$, which of the following could be $f(x)$?

(A) $f(x) = \dfrac{1}{5}x + \dfrac{1}{3}$

(B) $f(x) = \dfrac{1}{5}x + 3$

(C) $f(x) = \dfrac{1}{3}x + 5$

(D) $f(x) = 3x + 5$

(E) $f(x) = 5x + 3$

6. Which of the following is the graph of $f(x) = |x + 5|$?

(A)

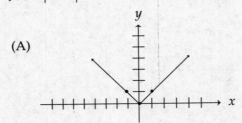

(B)

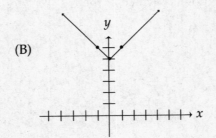

(C)

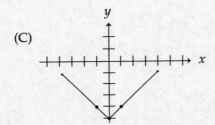

(D)

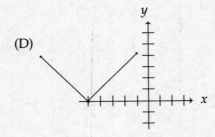

(E)

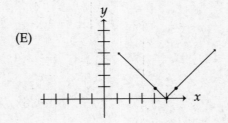

Arctic Sea Ice Draft Height by Region

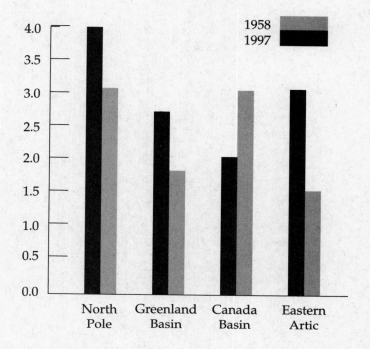

7. According to the chart above, in 1997, which Arctic region's ice drafts were approximately $\frac{2}{3}$ of their 1958 height?

    I. North Pole
   II. Canada Basin
  III. Eastern Arctic

(A) I only
(B) II only
(C) III only
(D) I and II only

(E) I, II, and III

HARD

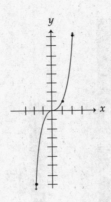

8. If the graph above shows $f(x) = x^3$, which of the following shows $f(x) = x^3 + 2$

(A) 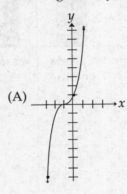   (B)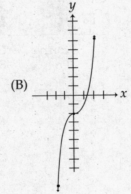

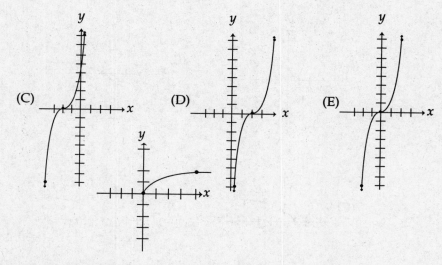

(C)   (D)   (E)

9. If the graph above shows $f(x) = \sqrt{x}$, which of the following shows $f(x) = \sqrt{x} - 1$?

(A)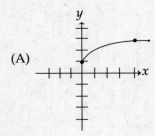

(B)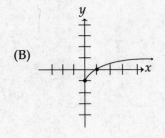

(C)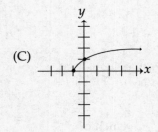

(D)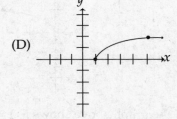

(E)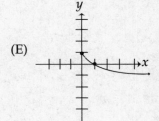

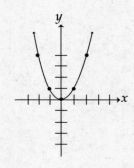

10. The graph above shows $y = x^2$. Which of the following represents $y = -x^2$?

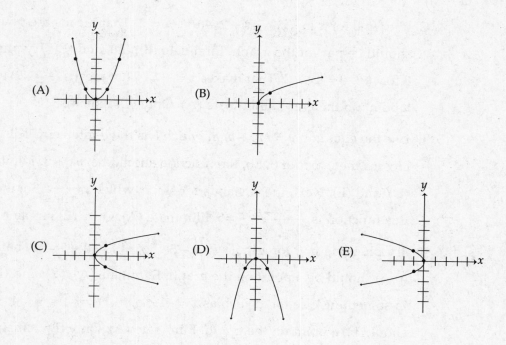

Answers and Explanations: Problem Set 18

1. **D** Remember that the formula for percent difference is $\dfrac{\text{difference}}{\text{original}} \times 100$.

   The discount provided at Store A is $\dfrac{5}{20} \times 100 = 20\%$. The discount

   provided at Store B is $\dfrac{5}{20} \times 100 = 25\%$, and the discount provided at Store

   C is $\dfrac{5}{30} \times 100 = 16\dfrac{2}{3}\%$. Only Stores A and B have a discount of 20% or

   more.

2. **B** Draw a line that connects most of the points. It is a straight line that goes down from right to left, which means it has a negative slope. Only (A) and (B) are negative slopes. Eyeball the line to see that it is not very steep. So, the slope is closer to 1 than 10. Alternatively, you could find points and ballpark the slope. The line roughly includes (50, 50), so the rise and run are the same. Therefore, the slope is −1.

3. **A** According to the data in the table, the temperature and the number of campers have a positive relationship at temperatures up to 85 degrees. That is expressed by an upward-sloping line. Above 85 degrees, the numbers have an inverse relationship, which is expressed by a downward-sloping line. Only graph (A) mirrors this relationship.

4. **C** Plug in 0 for x in $f(x) = 4x + 2$. $4(0) + 2 = 2$. That means the point $(0, 2)$ should be part of the graph. Eliminate (B), (D), and (E). Try plugging in 0 for $f(x)$. $0 = 4x + 2$. That makes $x = -\frac{1}{2}$. That means $(-\frac{1}{2}, 0)$ should be a point on the graph. Eliminate (A). Only (C) remains.

5. **E** Use the equation $y = mx + b$, in which b is the y-intercept. This function crosses the y-axis at 3. So, the function should be $mx + 3$. Eliminate (C), (D), and (E). Next, the m stands for slope, which is $\frac{\text{rise}}{\text{run}}$. So, the slope of this function is $\frac{3-(-2)}{0-(-1)} = \frac{5}{1} = 5$. Eliminate (A). Only (E) remains.

6. **D** Try plugging in 0 for x in $f(x) = |x + 5|$. So, $f(0) = |0 + 5| = 5$. That means $(0, 5)$ should be a point on the graph. Eliminate (A), (C), and (E). Plug in something else for x, such as $x = -1$. So, $f(-1) = |-1 + 5| = 4$. So, $(-1, 4)$ should be a point on the graph. Eliminate (A). Only (D) remains.

7. **B** Read the labels for both the year and the height of each ice draft, then determine which 1997 bar is $\frac{2}{3}$ of its corresponding 1958 bar. In 1997, the Canada Basin's ice draft measured 18; this is $\frac{2}{3}$ of its 1958 ice draft of 27.

8. **A** Try plugging in some values for x and see if the graphs include that point. If $x = 0$, then $y = (0)^3 + 2 = 2$. So, the graph should include $(0, 2)$. If $x = 1$, then $y = (1)^3 + 2 = 3$. So, the graph should include $(1, 3)$. If $x = -1$, then $y = (-1)^3 + 2 = 1$. So, the graph should include $(-1, 1)$. Only (A) includes these 3 points.

9. **B** Did you plug in? Plug in for x and see what happens. If $x = 0$, then $y = \sqrt{0} - 1 = -1$. So, the graph should include $(0, -1)$. If $x = 1$, then $y = \sqrt{1} - 1 = 0$. So, the graph should include $(1, 0)$. Only (B) fits these points.

10. **D** It's all about plugging in. If $x = 0$, then $y = -(0)^2 = 0$. So, $(0, 0)$ should be a point on the graph. If $x = 1$, then $y = -(1)^2 = -1$. So, $(1, -1)$ should be a point on the graph. If $x = -1$, then $y = -(-1)^2 = -1$. So, $(-1, -1)$ should be a point on the graph. Only (D) includes these three points.

PROBLEM SET 19: MIXED BAG

EASY

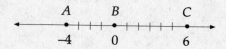

$$A \qquad B \qquad C$$
$$-4 \qquad 0 \qquad 6$$

1. On the number line above, what is
   $BC - AB$?

   (A) 0
   (B) 2
   (C) 4
   (D) 6
   (E) 10

2. If the hundreds digit and the tens digit of 5,425
   are reversed, the result is

   (A) 1,800 less than 5,425
   (B) 180 less than 5,425
   (C) equal to 5,425
   (D) 180 more than 5,425
   (E) 1,800 more than 5,425

MEDIUM

3. For a desktop, a cabinetmaker designed a
   border that consisted of a row of inlaid squares
   of different kinds of wood. If the border started
   with a square of oak and continued with cherry,
   walnut, ash, and maple, in that order, what kind
   of wood was the 83rd square?

   (A) oak
   (B) cherry
   (C) walnut
   (D) ash
   (E) maple

4. A, B, C, and D lie on a line. The distance
   between A and B is 12. Point B is the midpoint
   of AD, and point C is the midpoint of AB. What
   is the distance between C and D?

   (A) 6
   (B) 12
   (C) 18
   (D) 24
   (E) 36

5. If S is the set of the prime factors of n, and R is the set of the prime factors of $2n$, how many more numbers does set R contain than set S?

(A) $2n$
(B) n
(C) 2
(D) 1
(E) 0

Number of Households	Number of Dogs
1	0
5	1
2	2

Number of Households	Number of Cats
3	0
3	1
2	2

6. The tables above show the number of cats and dogs owned by the same 8 households. If the households that own either no dogs or 2 dogs also have no cats, then 2 households own

(A) no cats and no dog
(B) no cats and 1 dog
(C) 1 cat and no dogs
(D) 2 cats and 1 dog
(E) 2 cats and 2 dogs

HARD

7. How many distinct numbers between 1 and 40 contain the digit 2, the digit 3, or the digits 2 and 3?

(A) 12
(B) 16
(C) 20
(D) 24
(E) 26

8. Bob has a pile of poker chips that he wants to arrange in even stacks. If he stacks them in piles of 10, he has 4 chips left over. If he stacks them in piles of 8, he has 2 chips left over. If Bob finally decides to stack the chips in only 2 stacks, how many chips could be in each stack?

(A) 14
(B) 17
(C) 18
(D) 24
(E) 34

9. Conchata began a hike at an average speed of 3 miles per hour. Mariel started the same hike 2 hours later. If Mariel hiked at an average speed of 4 miles per hour, how many hours did it take Mariel to catch up to Conchata?

(A) 1
(B) 4
(C) 6
(D) 10
(E) 12

10. How many people must be in a group in order to be certain that at least 2 people in the group have first names that begin with the same letter?

(A) 20
(B) 26
(C) 27
(D) 35
(E) 64

ANSWERS AND EXPLANATIONS: PROBLEM SET 19

EASY

1. **B** BC has a length of 6. AB has a length of 4. So $BC - AB = 2$.

> **TIP:**
>
> On number line problems, sometimes you want the distance between 2 points, as in the problem above. And sometimes you want the number of a point on the line—for instance, using this number line, $A + B = -4$, because $A = -4$ and $B = 0$. You can have a negative value for a point on the line, but not a negative distance. Read the problem carefully and mark up your diagram so you don't confuse the two.

2. **B** This question really just tests your knowledge of decimal places. In the number 5,425, the digit 4 is in the hundreds place and the digit 2 is in the tens place. If we reverse these two digits, we get the number 5,245. We don't actually need to do any math to get the answer—just estimate. 5,245 isn't too far from our original number, so we can eliminate (A) and (E). In fact, it's just a bit less than our original number, so the answer is (B).

MEDIUM

3. **C** This is a pattern question, and you do them all the same way. How many elements are in the pattern? 5, in this case. Divide 5 into the total, which is 83. You get 16 with a remainder of 3. That means the whole pattern is repeated 16 times and continues 3 elements past that. Just count to the third element in the pattern, which is walnut.

> **TIP:**
>
> In a pattern question, don't convert the remainder of the division problem into a fraction. In other words, if the pattern has 3 elements, and the total is 7, your dividend should be 2 remainder 1, not $2\frac{1}{3}$.

4. **C** The easiest way to solve this problem is to draw a number line. Let's say that point A is at 0 on the number line and that B is at 12. Since 6 is the midpoint of AB, this puts C at 6. Therefore, the distance between C and D is $24 - 6$, or 18.

5. **D** Plug in. Let's say $n = 10$. The prime factors of 10 are 2 and 5. It has 2 prime factors. $2n = 20$. The prime factors of 20 are 2, 2, and 5. It has 3 prime factors. 20 has 1 more prime factor than 10. Plug $n = 10$ into the answers to find 1. Only answer (D) works.

> **TIP:**
> These questions are a bummer because sometimes it's hard to know where to begin. If you don't see any starting point, just try some numbers and see what happens. If you try a couple of different things and nothing seems to work, skip the question and come back to it later. These questions appear most often in the easy and medium sections. Depending on how the question is asked, you may be able to plug in.

6. **D** Do this one step at a time. There's only one household with no dogs. Draw a line from that household to the row with no cats. Then draw a line from the 2 households with 2 dogs to the households with no cats. We're left with the 5 households that have 1 dog—and on the other table, 3 households have 1 cat and 2 households have 2 cats. So 3 households have 1 cat and 1 dog, and 2 households have 2 cats and 1 dog.

> **TIP:**
> It's confusing, all these dogs and cats. It would be very easy to get the two categories mixed up. Just don't go too fast and start over again if you lose your grip.

HARD

7. **D** Write them all down, in an orderly fashion, one digit at a time. The numbers containing 2 are: 2, 12, 20, 21, 22, 23, 24, 25, 26, 27, 28, 29, 32. The numbers containing 3 are: 3, 13, 23, 30, 31, 32, 33, 34, 35, 36, 37, 38, 39. Not so fast! This is a hard question, remember? You need to check to see whether any numbers are repeated—and sure enough, 23 and 32 are on both lists. So cross off the duplicates, and *then* count up the numbers.

> **TIP:**
> On this kind of problem, don't try anything fancy. Just write down the list, being careful not to miss anything, and then count up how many you have. On a hard question, there's likely to be some kind of sneaky trap, as in the question above. Be wary.

8. **B** This is a remainder question. If the chips are in stacks of 10, there are 4 left over. That means there's a total of 14 chips, or 24, or 34, or any number × 10 with 4 added. If the chips are in stacks of 8, there are 2 left over, which means there are 10, 18, 26, or 34 . . . or any number × 8 with 2 added. 34 works for both 10-chip stacks with remainder 4, and 8-chip stacks with remainder 2. But the question asks for the number of chips in each stack, so you have to divide 34 by 2. You could also backsolve by dividing the answer choices first to get the total number of chips.

9. **C** It never hurts to make a little diagram:

Hours:	1	2	3	4	5	6	7	8
miles/Conchata:	3	6	9	12	15	18	21	24
miles/Mariel:	0	0	4	8	12	16	20	24

All we're doing is keeping track of their progress, hour by hour. Mariel catches up to Conchata at 24 miles, at which point Conchata had hiked for 8 hours and Mariel for 6. (They must be in pretty good shape.)

> **TIP:**
> You could solve this question by writing an equation based on the formula *rate* × *time* = *distance*, but it's much harder that way. You have to realize that the distance is equal and that Conchata's time is Mariel's time plus 2 hours, giving you the equation $3(x + 2) = 4x$. It's hard to come up with that kind of equation when you're under time pressure. We like the chart much better.

10. **C** In order to be certain, you have to allow for the worst case scenario—every person's name begins with a different letter. So the first person's name begins with A, the second with B, the third with C, etc. When you get all the way to Z, you have 26 people, so the 27th person's name will have to begin with a letter you already have, no matter what the letter is.

> **TIP:**
> Don't pick anything obvious. A lot of people are going to pick 26 for this question, because there are 26 letters in the alphabet. On a hard question, there's got to be more to it than that.

PROBLEM SET 20: GRID-INS

EASY

1. If $x - y = -6$, then y is how much greater than x?

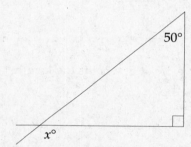

2. In the figure above, what is the value of x?

	Day 1	Day 2	Day 3
pies	15	12	10
cakes	6		
toys	16		15
hats	5	22	

3. The unfinished chart above shows the sales for a certain booth at a three-day fair. If, at the end of the fair, the owners of the booth sold more pies than toys, then how many toys could have been sold on Day 2?

4. If {x} is defined as the number of distinct prime factors of x, what is the value of {15} − {38}?

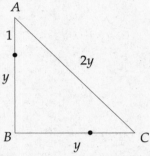

5. In the figure above, if y = 5, what is the length of BC?

6. If x is an integer, and $\frac{x}{4}$ less than .8 and greater than .25, what is one possible value of x?

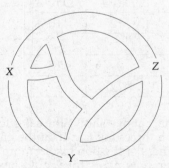

7. On the map above, X represents a theater, Y represents Chris's house, and Z represents Peter's house. Chris walks from his house to Peter's house without passing the theater and then walks with Peter to the theater without walking by his own house again. How many different routes can Chris take?

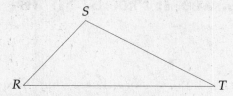

Note: Figure not drawn to scale.

8. Line *SV* (not shown) bisects *RT*, which has a length of 8. *SU* (not shown) has a length of 7, is perpendicular to *RT*, and bisects *RV*. Let *A* and *a* be the areas of *SVT* and *RSU*, respectively. What does $A - a$ equal?

TRANSPORTATION TO AND FROM WORKPLACE

Number of people

2000
1500
1000
500
0

walk   bus   car   subway

means of transportation

9. According to the chart above, what is the ratio of the number of people who walk to work to the number of people who do not walk to work?

10. In a certain game, 8 cards are randomly placed face-down on a table. The cards are numbered from 1 to 4 with exactly 2 cards having each number. If a player turns over two of the cards, what is the probability that the cards will have the same number?

ANSWERS AND EXPLANATIONS: PROBLEM SET 20

EASY

1. **6**

   Set the equation equal to y, since that's what the question asks for. You get $-y = -6 - x$. Multiply through by -1 and you get $y = 6 + x$, so the answer is 6. For an easier solution, you could also plug in here: Say $x = 2$ and $y = 8$, which satisfies the equation. Then y is equal to x plus 6.

2. **140**

   The unmarked angle in the triangle is 40°, since triangles have 180° and the other angles are 50° and 90°. The 40° angle and x lie on a straight line, so $40 + x = 180$, and $x = 140$.

3. **0, 1, 2, 3, 4, or 5**

   The total number of pies sold was $15 + 12 + 10 = 37$, and so far the number of toys sold was $16 + 15 = 31$. If they sold more pies than toys, they could sell anything from 0 to 5 toys and still be under 37. It doesn't matter which number you grid in.

MEDIUM

4. **0**

   The distinct prime factors of 15 are 3 and 5, so {15} is 2. (The function definition is the number of distinct prime factors. It doesn't matter what the factors are, just how many of them there are.) 38 has 2 distinct prime factors as well: 2 and 19. So {38} is 2. That means $\{15\} - \{38\} = 2 - 2 = 0$.

5. **8**

   As always, write the info on your diagram: If $y = 5$, then $AB = 6$ and $AC = 10$. Use the Pythagorean theorem to figure out BC, or notice that it's a 6:8:10 right triangle—either way, $BC = 8$.

6. **3 or 2**

Deal with the "less than" and "greater than" parts of this problem one at a time. Convert .8 to a fraction: It's $\frac{8}{10}$. Now try plugging in some numbers for x: If

$x = 1$, $\frac{1}{4}$ is less than $\frac{8}{10} \cdot \frac{2}{4}$ is less than $\frac{8}{10} \cdot \frac{3}{4}$ is less than

$\frac{8}{10}$. That's it—so far, x could be 1, 2, or 3. Now for the other part of the problem. Convert .25 to a fraction: it's

$\frac{1}{4} \cdot \frac{x}{4}$ has to be greater than $\frac{1}{4}$, so x can't be 1. But it could be either 2 or 3.

7. **6**

Here they are:

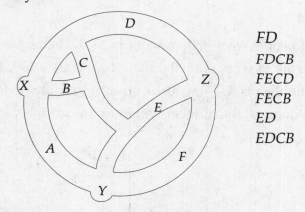

FD
FDCB
FECD
FECB
ED
EDCB

(You don't need to write in the extra letters—we just did it so we could show all the routes.)

This kind of question could keep you going forever, especially since it isn't even multiple choice. Do it a couple of times, grid in your best guess, and keep going. It's impossible to feel very secure about an answer to this type of question because you always feel like you're overlooking something. Don't worry about it—that's just the nature of the question.

8.   **7**

Draw the two new lines and write in the given lengths.
Your diagram should look like this:

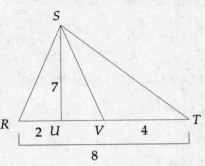

The altitude of both triangles is 7. So if the base of *SVT* is 4 and the
base of *RSU* is 2, *A* = 14 and *a* = 7. And as you most certainly know,
14 − 7 = 7. The whole trick of this question is reading carefully and
following the directions so your diagram is correct.

9.   **$\frac{4}{9}$ or .44 or .444**

The number of people who walk to work is 2000. The number of people
who do NOT walk to work is 1500 (bus) + 1000 (car) + 2000 (subway)
= 4500. The ratio then is $\frac{2000}{4500}$, which you could simply divide on your
calculator or reduce, so the number will fit on the grid.

10. $\dfrac{8}{56}$, $\dfrac{4}{28}$, or $\dfrac{1}{7}$

This is a little tricky: The first card doesn't matter, because the problem doesn't ask you to match a particular number, just any number. So the probability of picking any card is 8 out of 8, or $\dfrac{8}{8}$. Now for the second card, you want to match whatever you drew the first time. There are 7 cards left, and only 1 of them will match your first card, so there's a 1 out of 7 chance of picking it. $\dfrac{8}{8} \cdot \dfrac{1}{7} = \dfrac{8}{56}$, or $\dfrac{1}{7}$.

The other way to do this question is to write out all the possibilities. The cards are numbered 1, 2, 3, 4 and 1, 2, 3, 4. Taking each card one at a time, you can make a list of the 2 cards the player turns over:

1, 2	2, 3	3, 4	4, 1	1, 2	2, 3	3, 4
1, 3	2, 4	3, 1	4, 2	1, 3	2, 4	
1, 4	2, 1	3, 2	4, 3	1, 4		
1, 1	2, 2	3, 3	4, 4			
1, 2	2, 3	3, 4				
1, 3	2, 4					
1, 4						

Now count up the number of matches: 4. The total is 28. $\dfrac{4}{28}$ is $\dfrac{1}{7}$. Does that seem like it would take too long? It doesn't really, once you get going. Write them out in order, and don't backtrack.

PROBLEM SET 21: MORE GRID-INS

EASY

1. If $2x - 3y = 7$ and $y = 3$, then what is the value of x?

2. In the figure above, if $a = 170$, what is the value of b?

3. At a certain beach, the cost of renting a beach umbrella is $4.25 per day or $28.00 per week. If Kelly and Brandon rent a beach umbrella for 2 weeks instead of renting one each day for 14 days, how much money, in dollars, will they save?

MEDIUM

4. If $x^3 = 27$, then what does 5^x equal?

5. The "zip" of a number is defined as any positive integer raised to a power of the same number. For example, the "zip" of 2 is 2^2. What is the greatest possible value of the "zip" of 4 minus the "zip" of x?

	Game One	Game Two	Game Three
Jerry	1st	4th	
Elaine			2nd
Kramer			1st
George	3rd	2nd	

6. The unfinished chart above records the results of 3 card games played by Jerry, Elaine, George, and Kramer. All four players played in each game, and there were no ties. If a player receives 5 points for first place, 3 points for second place, 1 point for third place, and no points for fourth place, what is the highest possible number of points that Kramer could earn for all three games?

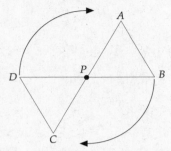

7. The figure above illustrates two fan blades in the shape of equilateral triangles that are rotated clockwise around Point P. How many degrees will the blades have rotated when Vertex D reaches the point where Vertex C is now?

HARD

8. In a certain cereal, the ratio of wheat flakes to raisins to almonds is 14:2:1. If $\frac{1}{4}$ cup of cereal contains 5 raisins, how many more wheat flakes than almonds are there in 2 cups of cereal?

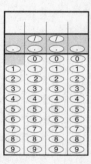

9. Seven neighbors who carpooled to work made a chart of the gallons of gas used by each member of the carpool during a certain time period. The number of gallons recorded on the chart were: 15, 10, 8, 8, 12, 14, and 17. The average number of gallons used was how much greater than the mode?

10. A cube with sides of 6 is split into 8 smaller cubes of equal size. What is the total length of the edges of the 8 smaller cubes?

ANSWERS AND EXPLANATIONS: PROBLEM SET 21

EASY

1. **8**

   The problem tells you that $y = 3$, so plug that into the equation and you get $2x - 9 = 7$. So $2x = 16$ and $x = 8$.

2. **10**

   Write $170°$ next to a. There are 180 degrees in a line, so $b = 10$.

3. **3.50**

   Kelly and Brandon spent $28 per week for 2 weeks for a total of $56. If they had rented the umbrella by the day, they would've spent $14 \times \$4.25$ for a total of $59.50. That means they saved $59.50 - 56 = 3.50$.

MEDIUM

4. **125**

   $x = 3$, and $5^3 = 125$.

5. **255**

   The "zip" of $4 = 4^4$, or 256 (use your calculator). If we're looking for the greatest possible value, we should subtract the smallest thing we can—we have to use a positive integer (it says so in the question) so let's use the "zip" of 1: $1^1 = 1$. So the "zip" of 4 (256) minus the "zip" of 1 (1) equals 255.

6. **13**

   In Game One, Kramer can't be 1st because Jerry is already 1st—so make Kramer 2nd. In Game Two, make Kramer 1st. Now count up Kramer's points: Game One: 3 points. Game Two: 5 points. Game Three: 5 points. That's a total of 13 points.

7. **300**

Draw a circle around the fan blades, so that the vertices lie on the circle. Now imagine that you've stuck a pin in Point P and are rotating the blades around, clockwise. When D hits where C is now, it's gone almost all the way around, hasn't it? The rotation is 360° minus the number of degrees in angle DPC, and since the blades are equilateral triangles, that's 60°, so the rotation covers 300°.

This would have been a good question to guess on—if you could tell that the rotation was between 180° and 360°, you might as well take a guess, since you won't lose any points for a wrong answer. Just guess quickly.

Hard

8. **260**

If there are 5 raisins in $\frac{1}{4}$ cup of cereal, there will be 40 raisins in 2 cups of cereal. ($\frac{1}{4} \times 8 = 2$ cups, and $5 \times 8 = 40$ raisins.) In the given ratio, the raisins were 2, and now there are 40. That means we need to multiply all the parts of the ratio by 20, since that's what we did to the raisins. That gives us a new ratio of 280:40:20, and all we have to do is subtract the almonds from the wheat flakes to get 260. Here's what your chart should look like:

$$\frac{\text{W : R : A}}{14 : 2 : 1}$$

$$\begin{array}{c|ccc} \frac{1}{4}\text{c.} & & 5 & \\ \hline 2\text{ c.} & 280 & : & 40 & : & 20 \end{array}$$

Sure, we could have figured out the wheat flakes and almonds in $\frac{1}{4}$ cup, but why bother—it would mean some ugly fractional messiness, and we might as well spend time dealing with 2 cups, since that's what the question wants anyway. Notice how a ratio can be multiplied by any number and still be the same ratio, as long as you multiply all the parts of the ratio by the same number, as we did here with 20.

9. **4**

   Do the average on your calculator: $15 + 10 + 8 + 8 + 12 + 14 + 17 = 84$, and $84 \div 7 = 12$. The mode is the number that shows up the most, so the mode is 8. All that's left is $12 - 8 = 4$.

   > **TIP:**
   >
   > Average, median, and mode questions tend to be pretty easy, even when they're in the hard section. The only trick is knowing what a mode and a median is. So learn how to find them—it's not complicated—and you'll be able to pick up some relatively painless points.

10. **288**

    It always helps to draw a diagram when they aren't nice enough to provide one. The original, uncut cube has sides of 6. If you divide it into 8 smaller cubes, the new sides will be 3. One cube has 12 edges, so the length of the edges of one cube is $3 \times 12 = 36$. Since you have 8 of these new cubes, multiply 36 by 8 and you get 288.

PROBLEM SET 22: MORE MIXED BAG

EASY

$$-6, -4, -2, 0, 2, 4, 6$$

1. How many different products can result from multiplying any two distinct numbers shown in the sequence above?

   (A) 8
   (B) 9
   (C) 10
   (D) 11
   (E) 12

2. If n and s are integers, and $n + 5 < 7$, and $s - 6 < -4$, which of the following could be a value of $n + s$?

   (A) 2
   (B) 3
   (C) 4
   (D) 6
   (E) 9

3. Line k and line j lie in the same plane and intersect once. If line p also lies in this plane, and it intersects line k once, which of the following must be true?

   (A) Lines k and j have the same slope.
   (B) Lines k and p have the same slope.
   (C) Lines j and p have the same slope.
   (D) Lines j and p do not have the same slope.
   (E) Lines k and p do not have the same slope.

MEDIUM

4. Which of the following lines is perpendicular to $y = 2x + 7$?

   (A) $y = 3x + \dfrac{1}{7}$

   (B) $y = 3x - \dfrac{1}{7}$

   (C) $y = -\dfrac{1}{2}x + 3$

   (D) $y = \dfrac{1}{2}x + 3$

   (E) $y = \dfrac{1}{2}x + 7$

5. $(-125)^{\frac{2}{3}} =$

   (A) $-83\frac{1}{3}$

   (B) -25

   (C) 25

   (D) $83\frac{1}{3}$

   (E) $5208\frac{1}{3}$

6. What is the area of an equilateral triangle with a side length of 10?

   (A) 25
   (B) $25\sqrt{2}$
   (C) $25\sqrt{3}$
   (D) 50
   (E) $50\sqrt{3}$

7. If d squared is inversely proportional to f raised to the fifth power, and the value of f is 2 when the value of d is 9, what is the approximate value of f when d is 4?

   (A) 1.78
   (B) 2.43
   (C) 2.77
   (D) 3.65
   (E) 7.93

HARD

8. The first term of a sequence of numbers is 2. Subsequently, every even term in the sequence is found by subtracting 3 from the previous term, and every odd term in the sequence is found by adding 7 to the previous term. What is the difference between the 77th and 79th terms of this sequence?

   (A) 11
   (B) 7
   (C) 4
   (D) 3
   (E) 2

9. Radioactive substance T-36 does not stay radioactive forever. The time it takes for half of the element to decay is called a half-life. If, before any decay takes place, there is 1 gram of radioactive substance T-36, and the half-life is 7 days, how much remains after 28 days?

   (A) 7^{-28}
   (B) 2^{-4}
   (C) 2^{-2}
   (D) 1^{-28}
   (E) 2^2

10. Kevin is unloading cargo from a truck into a warehouse. He has to move each of 20 packages up an incline set at 30°. If the floor of the truck is 2 meters lower than the floor of the warehouse, and Kevin has to carry each package separately, what is the total distance that Kevin covers on the incline to completely unload all 20 packages?

   (A) 200 meters
   (B) 160 meters
   (C) 80 meters
   (D) 40 meters
   (E) 20 meters

Answers and Explanations: Problem Set 22

Easy

1. **C** Nothing fancy here; just systematically multiply all of the numbers together. Start at one end of the sequence and work your way across, and remember you are only counting the distinct products. So, if you start on the left side with –6, (–6 × –4) = 24, (–6 × –2) = 12, (–6 × 0) = 0, and so on. Then when you finish with –6, start with –4 and work your way across: (–4 × –2) = 8, (–4 × 0) = 0, and so on. In the end, count up all the different products, and you should have 10.

2. **A** First fix the ranges. We see that $n < 2$ and $s < 2$. Since they both must be integers, the greatest either n or s could be is 1. 1 + 1 is 2, so that is the only answer that works.

3. **E** Any two lines that cross cannot have the same slope. Thus, k and j do not have the same slope, and neither do k and p. We unfortunately do not know anything about how j and p compare. All of this gets rid of (A) through (D), leaving only (E) left as the correct answer.

Medium

4. **C** In the form $y = mx + b$, m is the slope, which means that the line given by the equation $y = 2x + 7$ has a slope of 2. A line perpendicular to $y = 2x + 7$ will have a slope that is the negative reciprocal to 2. (C) has a slope of $-\dfrac{1}{2}$.

5. **C** Think of the whole number (–125) as a product. Within the fractional exponent, the denominator (3) gives the number of times some factor is used to make that base. Find the factor and raise it to the power in the numerator of the exponent (2). $-125^{\frac{2}{3}} = \left(\sqrt[3]{125}\right)^2 = (-5)^2 = 25$.

6. **C** In order to find the area, you need to find the height first. It's important to draw a picture. When you draw in the height, notice that it makes a 30:60:90 triangle, with the hypotenuse as 10, and the short side as 5. This must mean that the other side (the height) is $5\sqrt{3}$. Just remember that the area formula is: $\dfrac{1}{2}b \times h$, so it is $\dfrac{1}{2} \times 10 \times 5\sqrt{3} = 25\sqrt{3}$.

7. **C** Be careful here, though, because we are dealing with d squared and f raised to the fifth power. In this case, the x_1 is 81, y_1 is 32, and x_2 is 16. If we plug these values into our inverse variation formula, we get: $81 \times 32 = y_2 \times 16$. $\dfrac{2592}{16} = y_2 = 162$. Remember, though, that you have just found the second value of f to the fifth power. Take the fifth root of 162 in order to find (C), which is 2.77.

HARD

8. **C** Start by writing out the terms until you see a pattern: 2, –1, 6, 3, 10, 7, 14, etc. The difference between every other term is 4.

9. **B** Use the chart below to show the number of grams of T-36 remaining after 28 days.

Day	Grams of T-36
0	1
7	$\frac{1}{2}$
14	$\frac{1}{2} \times \frac{1}{2} = \frac{1}{4}$
21	$\frac{1}{2} \times \frac{1}{2} = \frac{1}{4} \times \frac{1}{2} = \frac{1}{8}$
28	$\frac{1}{2} \times \frac{1}{2} = \frac{1}{4} \times \frac{1}{2} = \frac{1}{8} \times \frac{1}{2} = \frac{1}{16}$

Since there is $\frac{1}{16}$ gram remaining after 28 days, you need to determine which answer equals $\frac{1}{16}$. Start with (C) and plug in the answers. $\frac{2^{-2}}{1} = \frac{1}{2^2} = \frac{1}{4}$. Try (B). $\frac{2^{-4}}{1} = \frac{1}{2^4} = \frac{1}{16}$. That's your answer!

10. **B** Make sure you draw a triangle to make this easier on you. In a 30:60:90 triangle, the smallest side (here 2 meters) is always half the hypotenuse. So the distance up the incline is 4 meters. He has to carry 20 packages up the incline, but he also has to walk back down each time to get another package. Therefore he does two trips on the incline for each package: 20×4 meters $\times 2 = 160$ meters.

NOTES

NOTES

Our Books Help You Navigate the College Admissions Process

Find the Right School

Best 366 Colleges, 2008 Edition
978-0-375-76621-3 • $21.95/C$27.95

Complete Book of Colleges, 2008 Edition
978-0-375-76620-6 • $26.95/C$34.95

College Navigator
978-0-375-76583-4 • $12.95/C$16.00

America's Best Value Colleges, 2008 Edition
978-0-375-76601-5 • $18.95/C$24.95

Guide to College Visits
978-0-375-76600-8 • $20.00/C$25.00

Get In

Cracking the SAT, 2008 Edition
978-0-375-76606-0 • $19.95/C$24.95

Cracking the SAT with DVD, 2008 Edition
978-0-375-76607-7 • $33.95/C$42.00

Math Workout for the NEW SAT
978-0-375-76433-2 • $16.00/C$23.00

Reading and Writing Workout for the SAT
978-0-375-76431-8 • $16.00/C$23.00

11 Practice Tests for the SAT and PSAT, 2008 Edition
978-0-375-76614-5 • $19.95/C$24.95

12 Practice Tests for the AP Exams
978-0-375-76584-1 • $19.95/C$24.95

Cracking the ACT, 2008 Edition
978-0-375-76634-3 • $19.95/C$24.95

Cracking the ACT with DVD, 2008 Edition
978-0-375-76635-0 • $31.95/C$39.95

Crash Course for the ACT, 3rd Edition
978-0-375-76587-2 • $9.95/C$12.95

Crash Course for the New SAT
978-0-375-76461-5 • $9.95/C$13.95

Get Help Paying for It

Paying for College Without Going Broke, 2008 Edition
978-0-375-76630-5 • $20.00/C$25.00

Available at Bookstores Everywhere
www.PrincetonReview.com

AP Exams

Cracking the AP Biology Exam,
2008 Edition
978-0-375-76640-4 • $18.00/C$22.00

Cracking the AP Calculus AB & BC Exams,
2008 Edition
978-0-375-76641-1 • $19.00/C$23.00

Cracking the AP Chemistry Exam,
2008 Edition
978-0-375-76642-8 • $18.00/C$22.00

**Cracking the AP Computer Science
A & AB Exams,** 2006–2007 Edition
978-0-375-76528-5 • $19.00/C$27.00

**Cracking the AP Economics (Macro &
Micro) Exams,** 2008 Edition
978-0-375-42841-8 • $18.00/C$22.00

**Cracking the AP English Language and
Composition Exam,** 2008 Edition
978-0-375-42842-5 • $18.00/C$22.00

Cracking the AP English Literature Exam,
2008 Edition
978-0-375-42843-2 • $18.00/C$22.00

**Cracking the AP Environmental
Science Exam,** 2008 Edition
978-0-375-42844-9 • $18.00/C$22.00

Cracking the AP European History Exam,
2008 Edition
978-0-375-42845-6 • $18.00/C$22.00

Cracking the AP Physics B Exam,
2008 Edition
978-0-375-42846-3 • $18.00/C$22.00

Cracking the AP Physics C Exam,
2008 Edition
978-0-375-42854-8 • $18.00/C$22.00

Cracking the AP Psychology Exam,
2008 Edition
978-0-375-42847-0 • $18.00/C$22.00

**Cracking the AP Spanish Exam,
with Audio CD,** 2008 Edition
978-0-375-42848-7 • $24.95/$29.95

Cracking the AP Statistics Exam,
2008 Edition
978-0-375-42849-4 • $19.00/C$23.00

**Cracking the AP U.S. Government
and Politics Exam,** 2008 Edition
978-0-375-42850-0 • $18.00/C$22.00

Cracking the AP U.S. History Exam,
2008 Edition
978-0-375-42851-7 • $18.00/C$22.00

Cracking the AP World History Exam,
2008 Edition
978-0-375-42852-4 • $18.00/C$22.00

SAT Subject Tests

**Cracking the SAT Biology E/M
Subject Test,** 2007–2008 Edition
978-0-375-76588-9 • $19.00/C$25.00

Cracking the SAT Chemistry Subject Test,
2007–2008 Edition
978-0-375-76589-6 • $18.00/C$22.00

Cracking the SAT French Subject Test,
2007–2008 Edition
978-0-375-76590-2 • $18.00/C$22.00

Cracking the SAT Literature Subject Test,
2007–2008 Edition
978-0-375-76592-6 • $18.00/C$22.00

**Cracking the SAT Math 1 and 2
Subject Tests,** 2007–2008 Edition
978-0-375-76593-3 • $19.00/C$25.00

Cracking the SAT Physics Subject Test,
2007–2008 Edition
978-0-375-76594-0 • $19.00/C$25.00

Cracking the SAT Spanish Subject Test,
2007–2008 Edition
978-0-375-76595-7 • $18.00/C$22.00

**Cracking the SAT U.S. & World History
Subject Tests,** 2007–2008 Edition
978-0-375-76591-9 • $19.00/C$25.00

Need More Than Math?

If you're looking to learn more about how to excel on the Math section of the New SAT, you're in the right place. Our expertise extends far beyond math or the New SAT. But this isn't about us, it's about getting you into the college of your choice.

One way to increase the number of fat envelopes you receive is to have strong test scores. So, if you're still experiencing some trepidation (Know what this means? Relax.), consider all your options.

We consistently improve students' scores through our books, classroom courses, private tutoring and online courses. Call **800-2Review** or visit *PrincetonReview.com*.

If you like our *Math Workout for the New SAT*, check out:
- *Reading and Writing Workout for the New SAT*
- *Cracking the New SAT*
- *11 Practice Tests for the New SAT and PSAT*
- *Cracking the ACT*
- *Cracking the SAT II: Math IC and IIC*